KU-472-302

TONY CURTIS
THE MAN AND HIS MOVIES

TONY CURTIS
THE MAN AND HIS MOVIES

Allan Hunter

PAUL HARRIS PUBLISHING
Edinburgh

IN THE SAME SERIES
Burt Lancaster: The Man and his Movies

HERTFORDSHIRE
COUNTY LIBRARY

2033343

Text © Allan Hunter 1985

No part of this publication may be reproduced, stored in a retrieval
system, or transmitted, in any form or by any means electronic,
mechanical, photocopying, recording or otherwise, without prior
permission of the publisher.

First published in Great Britain 1985 by
Paul Harris Publishing
40 York Place
Edinburgh

ISBN 0 86228 086 9 (cased)
ISBN 0 86228 087 7 (paper)

Designed by Charles Miller Graphics, Edinburgh
Typeset by Witwell Ltd., Liverpool
Printed by Billings & Sons Ltd., Worcester

CONTENTS

Acknowledgements

This book is a direct descendant of a similar venture, 'Burt Lancaster: The Man and his Movies', and I would like to thank Paul Harris for his continued enthusiasm and interest in this projected series.

As with any film work involving research I am deeply indebted to the various departments of the British Film Institute and National Film Archive. Their attentiveness and courtesy is always appreciated. I have read and used many articles and books incorporating material on Tony Curtis in preparing this book. Individual quotations from previous works are credited within the text and a bibliography of the more useful items is given at the close of the book.

The stills reproduced within this book were originally distributed to publicise the films and career of Tony Curtis, individual acknowledgement is offered within the text. My thanks are due to the respective members of the stills collections of the National Film Archive and the Kobal Collection.

The following individuals were of particular aid in writing this book; Maureen Day of Videospace, Sue Hausner of Slenderline Productions, Pat Kirkwood of the Kobal Collection, Jo Kulesza of J & M Film Sales, Verna Mitchell of the Larry Edmunds Bookshop in Los Angeles, Donna Moreno of Cannon Films, Jim Hickey, Director of the Edinburgh Film Festival, and the Recorded Picture Company.

Allan Hunter

THE MAN

Tony Curtis is a survivor. When he first arrived in Hollywood in 1948 few people would have rated his chances of still being employed as an actor thirty-five years later. Fewer still could have predicted that he would become one of the most popular stars of his generation receiving, at one stage, ten thousand letters per week requesting a lock of his hair. His early life reads like the most cliched of soap operas; a poor Jewish boy from the toughest neighbourhood of New York pulls himself up by his own bootstraps —ending up wealthy, sophisticated and successful. Curtis's life is far more complex and compelling as he has overcome personal setbacks and career depressions to develop into a bruised and battered older, and sometimes, wiser man. He has known tremendous acclaim that has allowed him to vindicate his private obsessions and satisfy his own diverse motivations, and he has also experienced crushing defeats that have almost stilled his fighting spirit. Yet he has always bounced back, ready to renew his quest for recognition and personal happiness.

He was born Bernard Schwartz in New York's Flower Hospital on June 3rd 1925. His father Mono or Manny Schwartz had been an amateur actor in Budapest before coming to New York with his wife Helen in search of the streets paved with gold that enticed so many European immigrants to the New World. In America Manny's poor command of the English language made acting work hard to come by and he turned to tailoring as a means of providing for his family. Young Bernie and his brothers Julius and Robert endured a childhood of grinding poverty and afterdark flittings to avoid the latest final demand from yet another irate rent collector. The family would hire a tailor's shop and use the space behind the shop as their living quarters. Every six months or so, when the payment of accumulated debts could no longer be postponed, the family quietly moved on, gaining another half year's breathing space. At one stage Bernie and Julius were accepted into a charity home for a month until their parents could fix up another temporary home.

In later years Curtis would recall with pride his father reciting the minutes at Hungarian Lodge meetings and happier family times sharing pots of goulash at Lodge picnics. However, his mother and father had different approaches to bringing up Jewish boys in the America of the Depression and there were often rows over his father's strict orthodox Judaism and his mother's more flexible beliefs. Tragedy struck when ten year-old Julius dashed onto a road running into an oncoming truck. Curtis felt responsible for his brother's death and, all his adult life, he has retained Julius's schoolbooks and cap.

Until he was six Bernard wore his hair in long plaits, payas, the symbol of his orthodox upbringing and an open invitation to a fight with the other youngsters on the block. He appears to have been a pugnacious youngster, more than capable of defending himself. The constant wanderings of his family always made him the new kid in town who had to prove himself. He developed a cocky bravado that showed to the neighbourhood that he was a youngster with whom it was best not to tangle. He would jump on the backs of moving vehicles to display his fearlessness and, in one incident, he leapt twenty-five feet from rooftop to rooftop in a spectacular stunt. A chimney interrupted his feat of daring and he was subsequently rushed to hospital with concussion, four broken ribs, temporary loss of hearing and double vision.

Later studio biographies would attempt to glamourise his years as a juvenile delinquent. In retrospect his acts as a youth had firmly placed him on the route to petty crime and more adult illegalities. Many of his street contemporaries wound up hardened criminals. Curtis credits truant officer Paul Schwartz with setting him on the straight and narrow. Schwartz took him to Jones Memorial Settlement House and, says Curtis, taught him; "honesty and self-respect." Aged twelve he became a Boy Scout and spent his summers at camp. He paid greater attention to his studies at Seward Park High School and also began to dream of a better life. His fantasies were fuelled by an insatiable

With his parents Mono and Helen Schwartz

appetite for the movies. "I was always crazy — nuts about movies", he told one reporter. "As a child I went to everything: Flash Gordon, Tarzan, the Dracula movies." He would stand in line for the dash and thrill of adventure films like 'Lives of a Bengal Lancer', 'Charge of the Light Brigade' and 'Beau Geste'. "You know my heroes as a kid? Cary Grant, Humphrey Bogart, Errol Flynn, Jimmy Cagney. Grant used to make me feel elegant when I walked out of the cinema, Bogart made me feel tough, Flynn made me feel dashing, Cagney made me feel cocky." He even began imitating his idols, sometimes with disastrous consequences. "I saw once in a movie that Errol Flynn bit into an onion. He chewed it and went on talking without even crying or flinching. I ate whole onions for a week steady. They ruined my nasal passages, my eyes and my ears. Not only that, nobody'd sit near me in the subway."

When America entered the Second World War Curtis joined the navy; he was six months short of graduating from high school. He served aboard the submarine U.S.S. Dragonette as a signalman. Whilst helping to load torpedoes in Guam a winch chain snapped and struck him. He lay in hospital for four weeks, his legs paralysed, and spent several months receiving medical treatment before he recovered and was discharged. The time had allowed him to ponder his future. After all he was not yet twenty and had some important decisions to take about what he intended to make of his life. He toyed with the idea of studying medicine and returned to New York to finish high school. Several events during the war years had convinced him that he should try his hand at acting. Aboard the USS Dragonette the crew had one film with which to entertain themselves —'Gunga Din' starring Cary Grant. Over the two years Curtis spent in the crew the film was played so often that the men could just cut the sound and enact the roles themselves. Curtis played Grant, furthering fostering his hero worship of the older star and instilling a certain desire to be like him. There was another motivating factor in his intention to enter the acting profession; "I fell in love with Hollywood when I went there as a young naval recruit. I had nowhere to sleep when I arrived but I remember the sign that lit up the sky bearing the suburb's name — only part of it wasn't working and it just said Ollywood; and I remember going to the Hollywood Canteen and hearing Gloria De Haven and Bette Davis entertaining the troops."

He decided to become an actor and made use of the G.I. Bill of Rights to enroll at the then burgeoning Dramatic Workshop in New York. As a war veteran Curtis was entitled to Government funds to subsidise educational opportunities. He was allowed a five hundred dollars a year allowance for tuition and books with an additional monthly allowance of fifty dollars to cover expenses. The Workshop was run by German-born Erwin Piscator and provided a variety of teachings that involved the students in all aspects of acting and stage presentation. Among the fellow luminaries of Bernard Schwartz in the immediate post-war period were Walter Matthau, Rod Steiger and Harry Belafonte.

He made his stage debut as the lighthouse keeper's idiot son in 'Thunder Rock' at New York's 92nd Street YMCA Playhouse. After a year at the Workshop he joined a stock company and toured the Borscht Circuit. His first professional work was with the Stanley Woolf Players, he took drama workshops with Walt Whitman and then he joined with a group of young actors who combined to form Empire Players, raised three hundred dollars to mount a production of 'Dear Ruth', opened in Newark and quickly went bust. He switched to the Cherry Lane Players and gained the leading role in a Greenwich Village production of Clifford Odets' 'Golden Boy'. One night the audience included Robert Goldstein, an East coast talent scout with Universal International studios. Goldstein was impressed and arranged an interview for the following Monday. Three days later Curtis was flown by luxury airliner to the film capital, met by a studio limousine and ushered to a plush hotel suite. With breathtaking haste it appeared that the young actor's dreams had all come true as if by the waving of a magic wand. The reality was rather different as Curtis would recall; "I felt like a King, sleeping late and having breakfast in bed. But all I had in the world was four dollars, twelve cents."

Curtis later described the Bernard Schwartz of 1948 as "a big bag of nothing put together with spit and glue." He was certainly unprepared for Hollywood; an unworldly young man whose naivety caused him great pain. Universal sensed in Curtis the raw material that could be groomed into star quality: he was five feet ten and a half inches tall, weighed one hundred and fifty eight pounds, had black, curly hair and piercing blue eyes; acting ability was not a prerequisite for his intended stardom. Universal was then engaged in establishing a resident company of promising young performers whom they hoped to groom for screen success. Among his contemporaries there were Rock Hudson and Piper Laurie. He was signed to a seven year contract with a starting salary of one hundred dollars a week, rising via six month renewal options to a princely fifteen hundred dollars weekly by 1955. In effect he became the property of Universal. They sent him to drama classes, voice lessons to smooth his rough and tumble Bronx tones, fencing lessons, horsemanship, pantomime and so on. They decided to change his name, firstly to Jimmy Curtis, then to Anthony, and finally Tony Curtis. They ensured that his name was mentioned in gossip columns and he was photographed meeting stars like James Stewart and Claudette Colbert.

Curtis found difficulty meeting the financial demands brought on by his new status. The studio advanced him a loan on his salary but he had to pay to join the Screen Actors Guild, he had to find accommodation, he needed to augment his meagre wardrobe and, with deductions, his first pay cheque amounted to seventeen dollars, eight cents. Initially he found a room, literally a mattress on a floor, for forty dollars a month, and later moved to a more luxurious rooming house for sixty-two dollars a month. He was hungry for success and hungry for more money. This need was matched by an inventive solution. To supplement his wages he secretly escorted tourists around the studio backlot in his pre-war Packard. He would charge two dollars a head and fabricate scandalous stories about the major stars. He also sold autographed photographs of Deanna Durbin that he had signed himself. "One day I went through the gate", he has said, "and I said to the cop, 'I've got some relatives', and the cop kinda half smiled at me as he flicked his eyes in the rear view mirror and I realised that three of my tourists were Chinese, and I was passing then off as my Uncle Irving and Aunt Silvia and so on."

U.S.S. Dragonette signalman Bernard Schwartz

He found it hard to make new friends and his defensively brash manner did little to endear him to his colleagues. His fellow workers would play practical jokes on him, locking him in steam rooms and dissolving sleeping tablets in his milk. On one occasion they waited for Curtis to go to work, completely emptied his apartment, changed the locks and let it to another tenant. Curtis was devastated when he returned home.

Curtis was quick to size someone up as friend or foe. Falling into the latter category was Universal talent coach Abner Biberman who would make fun of his Bronx accent and humiliate him in front of his fellow students. In the 1960s Curtis said; "He called me terrible names in front of the class and embarrassed me. He said I was a lousy actor, a punk out of New York. As soon as I saw the reactions I got in my first couple of movies I knew I would never have to go to that acting class again." Others in the film community warmed to the gauche young man. "When I first came to Hollywood I was really like a nature boy. You never saw such a left-footed, clumsy-looking bum. I'd never been in a private home. I didn't know what it was to have a private bathroom or what forks to use. Once I had dinner at Cole Porter's home and he had some beautiful glasses, obviously blown by an angel, just like paper. I was holding the glass in my hand and sure enough I broke it in fourteen pieces. The table was soaked with champagne. Ethel Merman was sitting right across from me and said: 'Kid don't worry about it.' With that, she grabbed her glass and crushed it into bits. I never forgot that."

He made his film debut in 'Criss Cross,' which was released in March 1949. He appeared in only a hundred feet of film, dancing with Yvonne De Carlo, and did not even receive a mention in the final credits. Studio bosses at Universal were stunned by reactions to his appearance and fan mail poured in addressed to 'that cute fellow who danced with De Carlo.' The studio rushed him into bit parts in several films and he made a strong impression as a mute killer in 'Johnny Stool Pigeon'. The fan mail grew and the studio realised that, with careful handling, they had a major star on their hands. In 1951 'The Prince Who Was A Thief' was a spectacular success, not only elevating Curtis to star status but also marking out his co-star Piper Laurie.

Early on Curtis realised the value of publicity and he was renowned for his cooperative attitude to both studio publicity stunts and fan magazine requests. He would pose for beefcake photographs — Tony at the beach, Tony and his cars, Tony and his yacht. He was a studio commodity who happily played ball with their demands in return for the rewards. The studio organised a competition to 'Win Tony Curtis for a Week'; unlucky competitors were allowed to talk to their idol by phone and, in the space of one hour, he chatted to a reported two hundred and forty five girls. The lady who did win him was rather disappointed as she had had her eye on the second prize — a gas cooker.

Now a star, Curtis wanted to visibly parade his new status and position within the Hollywood firmament. He was determined to enjoy all the trappings of wealth and to compensate for the deprivations of his childhood. His first priority was to replace his antiquated Packard. He borrowed a thousand dollars from his agents for the down payment on a brand new silver-grey Rolls-Royce. "It was a symbol. I wanted it because it was something that I could wear as a badge to stick my nose at other actors who weren't doing as well and say; 'Look how goddamned successful I am.' I wanted to get back at a lot of people in Hollywood who gave me a hard time when I got started." Over the ensuing years he indulged himself in all the traditional material symbols that are equated with success — fast cars, snappy clothes and beautiful women. He built up a wardrobe of thirty Italian suits, forty-four silk shirts with special collars two inches higher than normal, four dozen pairs of shoes and four dozen pairs of imported socks.

During one Hollywood party he met Janet Leigh, a fast-rising young actress who had already been married twice. Born Jeanette Helen Morrison in Merced, California on July 26th 1927, she had studied music at the College of the Pacific and eloped, aged fifteen, with nineteen year old John Carlyle. The marriage was annulled after a few months. At college she met bandleader Stanley Reames and they were married on October 5th 1946. Her father worked in insurance and real estate and, during the summer of 1946, her mother was employed as a receptionist at the Sugar Bowl Ski Lodge in Soda Springs. A doting mother, she kept a picture of her daughter on her desk. It attracted the attention of one of that season's tourists —retired actress Norma Shearer who sent the photo to her former studio, MGM, and enclosed a letter suggesting they give the girl a screen test. Reames wanted to try the band scene in Los Angeles and so the newly wed Mrs Reames left college and headed for Hollywood. Much to her surprise she was hired and Mrs Jeanette Reames became Janet Leigh, film actress. She recalled; "I was simply flabbergasted when they offered me one of those routine starlet contracts, but I was so happy to get that fifty dollars a week. We were living over my aunt's garage and the money was welcome. I knew I couldn't act, but they promised to give me dramatic lessons, and the first picture I tested for was 'The Romance of Rosy Ridge' opposite Van Johnson. I'd only had a few lessons and, when they told me I had the part, I said, 'You can't make me do that. You promised to teach me to act.' They were looking for a green, naive, unsophisticated girl for that picture and they sure found one." Over the next few years she appeared with Walter Pidgeon in 'If Winter Comes' (1947), played Greer Garson's niece in 'That Forsythe Woman' (1949) and co-starred with Robert Mitchum in 'Holiday Affair' (1949). When she met Curtis in 1950 she had been divorced from bandleader Reames for two years. The couple were instantly attracted and planned to marry; a union that was strongly opposed by Universal who claimed that having Curtis a married man would ruin his sex appeal with the teenage fans. Nevertheless the couple eloped and were married at Greenwich, Connecticut on June 4th, 1951 — the day after Curtis's twenty-sixth birthday.

Curtis and Leigh shared many characteristics — both were attractive young stars, both the virtual creations of their respective studios (Universal and MGM), and both ambitious for success. They became the Douglas Fairbanks and Mary Pickford of the teen set and even moved into a lavish mansion next to Pickfair in Beverly Hills. Fan magazines clamoured for the merest whisper of their latest activities and the couple were only too happy to oblige, attending all the right parties and premieres, posing for photographs and giving endless interviews. The fan magazines responded by gushing approval. An extract from the Screen Parade of February 1952 gives an example of the kind of reports that the public were apparently dying to read: "He drinks no hard liquors, smokes less than a pack of cigarettes a day, works out daily, is an excellent boxer, wears no rings, lunches on steak and orange pop, spells badly, jitterbugs like a champion but stumbles on a tango, collects jazz records, will drive fifty miles to see an old Marx Brothers comedy and numbers among his closest friends Jerry Lewis, Marlon Brando and anyone Janet thinks is nice." They won the 'Golden Apple' from the Hollywood Women's Press Club as the most co-operative stars. Curtis was given the Foreign Press's 'Henrietta Award' as the most promising actor and named a 'Star of Tomorrow' in 1953. Both were heavily worked in an indiscriminate range of films, sometimes appearing together, but with little say in the direction of their careers. To the press and the fans it seemed a dream marriage of two happy, attractive, successful people — they were Hollywood's perfect young couple. The reality of the situation was something altogether different.

The ticket-buying public and the fan magazines may have loved Curtis as the dashing, often improbable, hero but the critics sneered. Curtis desperately wanted the esteem that Cary Grant had, and the critics' jibes ruined his fragile self-confidence. He had no measure of his own worth and relied excessively on other peoples' opinions of what he was doing. He wanted to be liked and he wanted to be accepted so he did what the studio thought best. Looking back in 1965 Curtis would say; "I was the Baron of Beefcake. I was a sort of billboard and they just pasted labels on me. I was a jerk. Little Bernie Schwartz who crawled out of a trash can in the Bronx. Don't ask me how I made it but I got there.

"I wanted to act and I had nothing. No education. No experience. They dressed me up and the critics murdered me because of my accent and they gave me a hairstyle and the fan magazines even ran a Win Tony Competition. I slayed the English language and I made money. That guy was a phoney but I like him. In fact I saw a couple of those early films on TV the other week and he wasn't as bad as the critics made him out considering what he was and what he was pretending to be. He tried to be what everybody wanted him to be. I was ashamed of myself. Imagine that! I tried to talk good, I tried to do what everybody told me. I wasn't true to myself."

In 1955 he appeared in several popular films and learnt that Janet was expecting their first child. He had wealth, fame and a good marriage, indeed more than Bernie Schwartz from the Bronx could have imagined in his wildest dreams. Yet he was unhappy; haunted by unfounded fears and pitifully lacking in self confidence. Janet went on location to Africa for a film called 'Safari' and he was so lonely and full of self-doubt in her absence that he insisted that any future films she made on location would be with him or not at all. Some Hollywood columnists reflected on the negative side of their partnership, one saying; "They were fearfully ambitious kids, so determined to make it, they were tiresome", another called them; "over eager, over nice, over everything." Curtis began seeing a psychiatrist hoping to reassess his approach to his life and career.

From the late 'Fifties onwards Curtis went through a period of private and professional transition. His acting reached maturity with a string of compelling performances in 'Sweet Smell of Success' (1957), 'The Defiant Ones' (1958) and 'The Outsider' (1961). He revealed a remarkably fine comedy talent in 'Some Like It Hot' (1959) and 'Operation Petticoat' (1959) with Cary Grant. He was earning twenty-five thousand dollars a week and the critics who once sneered now applauded and revised their opinions. He was nominated for an Academy Award as Best Actor and reached new heights as a box-office attraction making the list of top ten stars twice at number six in 1960 and number nine in 1961. In 1957 and 1960 he was voted special Golden Globe awards as a World Film Favourite. It was the most rewarding period of his career, yet such an unbroken string of professional successes masked considerable turmoil in his private life.

His parents had instilled him with many notions and he recalled; "My parents were very superstitious. They taught me that if something good happened you were always going to get paid off." During this period when nothing but good things seemed to happen Curtis was continually looking over his shoulder awaiting the concomitant pay-off. Between 1955 and 1959 he spent thirty thousand dollars on analysis and sometimes visited his

Beverly Hills psychiatrist as often as four times a week. "My analysis was the first sign of my need to find out about myself", Curtis said. "There was something missing. I wasn't getting enough stimulation in my life. I thought it was wonderful to have somebody to tell those dark and dreadful things I had never told anybody, someone to finally listen to all my problems. To get somebody to be concerned only about me for fifty-five minutes was terrific. How often do you get that in a normal conversation. I would have spilled my guts to anybody with a receptive ear."

During his years of stardom Curtis had displayed many eccentricities that were more than just star temperament. Firstly there was his attitude to the famous Tony Curtis haircut which influenced a whole generation of youths. "The Tony Curtis haircut was a phoney. It all began because I couldn't afford a haircut", he said. "Then I thought my very gift was something so mystical and magical that by cutting my hair I thought it would be gone. I could understand what Samson felt. I was afraid if they cut my hair too much they would cut my talent." He was superstitious and almost paranoid about his career; "I was afraid people in the industry were trying to ruin my career. I was suspicious of everybody. I was certain that someone was trying to bust my contract or steal parts from me. They were laying for me outside like in the old Chicago gangster movies. I had nothing but my career and therefore it made me frightened." His fear spilt over into many areas. He felt a continued obsession that he might die in a plane crash, and refused to fly anywhere. "I didn't want to take a chance of falling down in an airplane and ending everything I had worked for. I didn't trust the pilot. Anywhere I went by boat, train or pack mule. I went to Argentina for Taras Bulba and I never got forty feet off the ground. It was written into every contract that I would not fly to a location. So if a studio wanted me badly enough they'd take me without flying. I was even using that as a club. It was my way of making it difficult for a studio. I would say: Let's see how much they really wanted me."

He also had a massive complex about status, his standing in the Hollywood community, and a fierce competitiveness that marred many of his personal relationships. "I was constantly playing the movie star part. I wanted everybody to think I was a wonderful fella. I couldn't wait to have visitors come on the set and watch me work. I was showing off for the crowd. And I looked forward to anybody remarking how terrific I was." He was briefly in with the Rat Pack crowd — Sinatra, Dean Martin, Sammy Davis Jnr and company. He gave lavish parties — hiring yachts and strolling gypsy players to impress his colleagues. When he discovered that Burt Lancaster and Kirk Douglas were learning to play golf he joined two golf clubs, practised with a frenzied compulsion to improve his game until his handicap was better than theirs then gave up golf. "I felt like a man; to be included in this circle was a wonderful feeling for me. But I didn't feel comfortable for some reason", he said.

In a revealing article by Richard Warren Lewis for Photoplay magazine, Lewis wrote; "Curtis was relying on the supernatural to protect himself against imagined adversity. The number nine whose shape fascinated him, and the number eight, which duplicates the sign for infinity when laid on its side, became critical in his thinking. He refused to attend business meetings unless they were scheduled at the hours of eight or nine in the morning or evening. Wednesday, the fourth day of the week and half of the number eight, was considered the ideal day for making decisions."

Curtis's years in analysis helped to lay to rest the ghosts of many of his fears and paranoias. Certainly there are explanations for his irrationality —the insecurity of his childhood and the jungle-like atmosphere of Hollywood had done little to bolster his self-confidence. Anywhere else he would have appeared as a spoilt brat showing off to impress his peers. In Hollywood, where major stars are at liberty to be eccentric because they are such a rare breed, his behaviour was tolerated and probably regarded as nothing too out of the ordinary.

The studio had always been there to protect and re-assure him as long as he was enticing the public to his films. Through his analysis he began to realise the need to take responsibility for his own actions and realise his own ability as a performer regardless of the good or bad impressions that others had of him. In the 'Sixties he was able to reflect on how the studio had cosseted him. A decade earlier he had become something of a hypochondriac suffering from many, probably psychosomatic, ailments — insomnia, back-ache, fatigue, and a dyspeptic stomach. Later he believed; "I was finding excuses for myself because I had little but my good looks to contribute in those days. Nobody cared whether I could act or not. I'd get on the set to do a scene and I'd have trouble with the dialogue. If it took more than four takes, the director would stop and say, 'Don't worry about it, kid, we'll change it'.

"Change it? That's the worst thing in the world you can do to a man. It was always made easier for me. I was never allowed to fight my way through anything. If a scene called for a rainstorm they'd warm up the water. I wasn't given the simple joy of getting wet and shivering. And I wasn't that skilled an actor that I could fabricate it".

As an actor he learnt by 'doing' and he improved immeasurably as he gained experience and maturity. Unfortunately for his self-esteem he had been allowed to make his early mistakes in a very public arena — motion pictures. His analysis helped him as a performer and he set to pleasing himself and achieving what he was capable of. Nevertheless, he has continually resented the absence of any recognition from the American Academy of Motion Picture Arts and Sciences. With a string of excellent performances from 'Sweet Smell of Success' to 'The Boston Strangler' he does have a point of some validity. "I'll tell you something", he said in a 1965 Sunday Express interview, "Once you're branded a lousy actor it's terribly hard to convince people otherwise. It damn near broke my heart when I got no recognition for 'The Defiant Ones' and 'Sweet Smell of Success'. I thought I wasn't bad in them but nothing happened. Nothing! If I'd come from the same distinguished theatrical background as Brando I'd have been nominated for awards for both films, I'm sure.

"I was so depressed about it that my agent, a great man called Lew Wasserman, took me to New York. First we went to the public library to borrow a book on acting by Stanislavsky, then we went to the New York Times and he had them pull out reviews of Grant, Gable and Cagney in the thirties — all of them my idols. 'If you still feel depressed after reading these notices', he said, 'you can start on the book.' Well, I tell you, I couldn't believe it. Their notices were diabolical. They had all been slaughtered in their early days. I handed the book back to him next morning. He didn't say anything." Also in 1965 he was able to say; "I just want to be as good an actor as I possibly can. I'm no Larry Olivier and I used to cry to be like him and to be able to act like him and speak like him. But that as they say is absurd. I am what I am and I'm happy."

From now on he prized honesty in a person above all else, and whilst he kept many of the trappings of his success it seemed to be for the pleasure he derived from them rather than to impress the neighbours and colleagues. One casualty of the 'new Curtis' was his marriage to Janet Leigh. They had had two daughters, Kelly Lee born on June 16th 1956 and Jamie Lee born on November 22nd 1958. Hollywood's perfect young couple were however far from happy. It was no secret that Leigh had constantly subordinated her career to the demands of being Mrs Tony Curtis and there were reports of rows both on the films they made together and in private. Leigh found far better film roles when she didn't co-star with Curtis as her performances in Orson Welles' 'Touch of Evil' (1958) and Alfred Hitchcock's classic 'Psycho' (1960) revealed. She had been nominated for the Oscar as Best Supporting Actress in the latter film. During the summer of 1961 Leigh, without Curtis, went on holiday to the riviera with the Kennedy family. She returned to America when her father committed suicide leaving a note blaming marital problems for his decision to take an overdose. Curtis and Leigh officially separated in March 1962 after almost eleven years of marriage. Within a few days Leigh was discovered in a coma in a New York hotel room after a reputedly accidental overdose of tablets. In the divorce settlement she was awarded custody of the children, and a Rolls Royce, a Cadillac, fifty per cent of the couple's cash, stocks, bonds, and oil properties, and one dollar a year alimony. She obtained a quick divorce in Mexico and married stockbroker Robert Brant in September 1962. Within six months Curtis was also remarried.

Looking back on this marriage Curtis said, "My first marriage was supposed to be the happiest in Hollywood. It wasn't. My marriage was hopeless and people were saying you can't let it go bust. One character even said: 'Where am I going to go for dinner if you two divorce?'. Janet is married again and she's happier and the kids are. She's married to a great guy and I don't resent the fact that my kids look up to him and treat me as a happy-go-lucky uncle. If I'd stayed on as I was they would have maybe made an idol of me and then found the feet of clay." A particular comfort to him at the time of the break-up was the sympathetic ear of his idol Cary Grant, now a close friend and confidante.

Whilst filming Taras Bulba in Argentina he fell in love with his leading lady, teenager

With his second wife Christine Kaufman   The Kobal Collection

Christine Kaufmann. Gossip columnists suggested that his relationship with Christine had caused the final split with Leigh but the couple seemed destined for divorce. They had been living a marriage that was latterly more for other people (the fans, the press etc) than for themselves.

Christine Kaufmann, born in Landsdorf in Austria on January 11th, 1945, had known little other than life as a film actress since childhood. Her French-born mother acted as their chaperone and the couple were married at the Riviera Hotel in Las Vegas on February 8th 1963 with Kirk Douglas as best man. Curtis was thirty-seven, Christine had just turned eighteen.

For a while Curtis seemed to have finally got everything in perfect harmony; he had adjusted to his success, was handling his career well and was devoted to his pretty young bride. The couple worked together on the comedy 'Wild and Wonderful', and Curtis became a proud father of two daughters, Alexandra and Allegra. He admitted; "She's good for me and I love her. You can see that Christine and I are happy. Ten years ago if I had met her as she is now she wouldn't have given me a glance." Hollywood noted Curtis's new confidence and honesty emerge in his approach to business. Sometimes he was honest to the point of being blunt. During the making of 'Some Like It Hot' he had been continually frustrated by the problems of working with Marilyn Monroe. In later years when asked about filming with the legendary Monroe he would reply; "I suppose the thing I most respect in anyone is honesty. I try to be honest myself. Always, people have said to me: 'Wasn't it a terrible tragedy about Marilyn Monroe?'. Well, I can't lie. I didn't like her. She was a really mean person. During 'Some Like It Hot' she gave us a terrible time. When someone asked me then what it was like kissing her, I said 'It's like kissing Hitler'. Paula Strasberg nearly fainted. I think Marilyn was mad as a hatter. She had a woman's body but the mind of a four-year-old. If she hadn't had that sexy look and thirty-eight inch bust she'd have been locked up, for sure. She sent Billy Wilder crazy during that film yet today he has nothing but nice things to say about her.

"I called him on it. 'How can you completely negate everything you said?', I asked. 'What's the point of knocking her now?', he replied. But I can't be like that. She was so awful. Marilyn and I knew each other when we arrived in Hollywood in 1948 and we were together for two or three months. And I can say for sure, the industry didn't do her in: it was the people around her. A studio doesn't make you nuts. Admittedly they try and intertwine your movie life and your social life but if you know how to handle yourself you survive."

Curtis began to use his muscle as a star to positively affect his career. He became more selective and worked less indiscriminately. He was supposed to be in 'The Unforgiven' (1960) with Burt Lancaster but relinquished the secondary role to Audie Murphy. In 1961 MGM signed him to appear in 'Lady L' but his contract included script approval and, when he didn't like what was happening to the script, he walked out leaving director George Cukor and co-star Gina Lollobrigida out in the cold. Asked to name a prime advantage of success he replied; "The ability to turn down things you don't want to do. For instance, I sent back quarter of a million dollars because I decided I didn't want to make the film about Playboy magazine. And I refused to go ahead with the original version of 'Lady L' even though they'd paid me four hundred thousand dollars while hanging about waiting for it to start. In those days it was a terrible script. I just couldn't do it. So I bought one share in MGM stock and threatened to sue as a minority stockholder for mismanagement of the studio unless they released me from the contract. They did". Lady L was finally filmed in 1965 with Sophia Loren and Paul Newman as co-stars and Peter Ustinov as director.

Curtis the candid was also level-headed about growing older; "I'm just forty", he said in 1965, "and I have to dye my hair for the parts I play so I know I'm getting on. Odd how preoccupied we are with youth really. There's nature very kindly giving us grey hair to soften the wrinkles on the face and we're busy dying it dark again which only points it up. The only secret I know for remaining youthful is to marry someone young, as I did. Though there are other ways. An actress I know has certainly found one. When I filmed with her years ago I was thirty one and she was thirty six. Today I'm forty and she's still only thirty-seven."

The seemingly contented Curtis reached another of his periodic crisis points in 1967. Throughout the 'Sixties he had forsaken the previous span of material he had once appeared in to concentrate almost exclusively on light comedy. In the 'Fifties he had made comedies as well; but interspersed with swashbucklers, drama, even a western and a musical. In 1967 'The Chastity Belt' was his ninth consecutive comedy film. Curtis does work well in comedy; he has an engaging personality, good timing, and a readily identifiable persona of the wheeler-dealer with the beguiling charm of a master con man. However, his choice of vehicles was not particularly wise: 'Goodbye Charlie' (1964) and 'Sex and the Single Girl' (1964) were successful but the response to his work after that was progressively poorer. By 1967 he had made a string of flops and, the following year, Variety included him in a list of stars that were considered over-priced in the light of recent box-office performances. In 1967 his marriage to Christine ended and he was facing a testing time. With typical panache he pulled himself back up to the top.

In Hollywood Twentieth Century-Fox were casting the part of mass murderer Albert De Salvo known as The Boston Strangler, a man accused of strangling thirteen women between June 1962 and January 1964. Curtis believed that the part was meant for him and was determined that no-one else would play the role. Hollywood insiders scoffed at the idea of 'pretty boy' Curtis as the Strangler. "I had to go on my knees to Twentieth Century-Fox to get the role. I've spent a fortune myself on headshrinkers, hypnotists and the like, so I thought I knew a little about things that go adrift in a man's mind. I also wanted to prove that an actor can still be attractive and have acting talent." Eventually Curtis wore a false nose and brown contact lens to disguise his blue eyes. He had worked on his own make-up, taken twenty-four pictures of himself and sent them to Richard Fleischer the intended director of the film. "I wanted to play De Salvo so much that I'd have spent three years in jail as compensation", the actor reported. When he was finally cast as De Salvo he immersed himself completely in the role. Divorced from Christine he was unattached for the first time since 1951 and ruthlessly dedicated to a role crucial to his career and his life. "I became De Salvo, I could no longer believe in Tony Curtis. It was a sort of purging for me.

For years I have wanted to find myself, to assess what might have happened to me if I hadn't been taken up by Hollywood. I might have been on the wrong side of the law myself. By doing this film I knew myself. I lost my anger, I became tolerant. It isn't so much that I became sympathetic with De Salvo. But I got what I call empathy with him. Here was a man whose life became a cul-de-sac. And I count myself lucky that I found the open road in time."

In 'The Boston Strangler' Curtis gives a remarkable performance, one that should have revitalised his career, and for a while he was riding on the crest of another wave. In 1969 he could tell the press; "Professionally it has been fabulous for my reputation in spite of a lot of letters I get from nuts who write, 'You're not the Boston Strangler I am'." He announced that he had purchased the rights to a book about Chicago gangster Bugsy Siegel and explained; "I am asked in my profession to do primarily comedy but I have not really explored the side of me that did 'The Defiant Ones' and 'Sweet Smell of Success'. I want to do very deep and mystical roles, like Tyrone Power in 'The Razor's Edge'. That was an examination of a man trying to find himself, showing the dark areas as well as the light and airy ones. I've found both of these in my own life and I'm very anxious to do them professionally. But until the Boston Strangler nobody would ask me to do that." For the moment his career seemed to have regained its momentum although he was again disappointed that his work went unrecognised by the various award-giving bodies when it came to acknowledging the year's best performances.

During the location filming of 'The Boston Strangler' he met and married twenty-four year old model Leslie Allen. By now he was living in the lap of luxury. One report listed his wealth running to oil wells in Texas, fleets of cars, six garages and two forty roomed apartment houses in Los Angeles. The once gaudy extravagances of his wardrobe had long since given way to the best and most fashion conscious styles. In 1970 the Men's Fashion Association voted him the Best Dressed Man of the Year. He had developed an interest in the art world and was a gifted amateur artist himself. The 'nature boy' who had arrived in Hollywood in 1948 had soaked up refinement and knowledge over the years and was now an art connoisseur and collector. He explained his passion for art to the Hollywood Reporter once; "I bought Joseph Cornell's boxes years ago when they weren't fashionable or talked about. I liked them so I bought some for seven hundred and fifty dollars and today many are worth forty thousand dollars or more. They reached me, I wanted to live with them. That's collecting, although I had no idea they'd be that valuable. A painter who was living abroad, John Levee, and Jules Stein's brother, David, who's in Paris, introduced me to the world of art. Through John's opening of some art gallery doors I bought three thousand dollars worth of lithographs and etchings, signed by Picasso, Chaghall, Miro... That was in 1956 when prices were on another scale. Billy Wilder also taught me to collect; I observed the objects, boxes, small screens he and Audrey lived with. Naturally, collecting art has led to collecting furniture, and art influences the way I live, one's personal behaviour as well; it's a never ending growth process. As far as I'm concerned, collecting helps a man or woman to establish an identity. I know myself better because of the things I've surrounded myself with." Among the other items he had surrounded himself with were an antique Swiss armoire, English period pieces and canvases by Alechinsky.

He claimed that his life-style was influenced by his idols Cary Grant and Leslie Howard. "As a child I was fascinated by the way Howard handled himself on the screen. He had such poise. But the luxuries cannot come until you've paid certain prices for them. Elegance is going through all the inelegance of life and finding out why it is. Giving up the easy way and making it the hard way is elegant. It's finding things that make you happy you're a man." Of all the major stars Curtis has certainly paid in full for the many luxuries in his life and in 1968, with his career back in first gear and the hopes of a new marriage to sustain him, it finally seemed as if this time everything had come up roses. Curtis himself seemed to be expressing some relief when he stated; "I'm not running any more. I can stand still and look around. I've been kissed by the gods. Now I am more my own man".

The films made by Curtis immediately following 'The Boston Strangler' were all flops. There was no-one coming forward to finance the Bugy Siegel film and, with the release of films like 'Easy Rider' and 'Midnight Cowboy' in 1969 making stars of Dustin Hoffman and Jack Nicholson, Curtis was beginning to look like yesterday's leading man. When Hollywood went through one of its cyclical slumps at the beginning of the 'Seventies there were fewer offers. He accepted one offer for a television series in Europe called 'The Persuaders', co-starring Roger Moore. In Britain the series was popular but it flopped badly in the all-important American market. In 1972, now a British resident, he was announced for a film called 'Another Day, Another Dollar'. It was never made. Within a few years the revitalising effect of The Boston Strangler had been dissipated. Understandably discouraged by the whole business he announced his retirement from the big screen. He chose to diversify, saying he would work for television, planned to write and, more immediately, hoped to make his Broadway debut in a new play 'Turtlenecks'. Furthermore, he told The Times in 1973: "I am going to take no more crap from anyone. I have spent twenty-five years in the clink (film industry). I won't make a feature film for anyone except myself. I won't expose myself to any outside influence. I have paid the piper". As a mark of his continued personal popularity he received thousands of fan letters begging him not to quit the movies.

His immediate energies were channelled into 'Turtlenecks', his first stage work since before beginning his film career. The play was partly financed by Curtis's friend Hugh Hefner of Playboy Productions and Curtis was to receive between seven and nine thousand dollars a week. If successful he hoped to tackle some classical roles citing Mark Anthony, Richard III and Malvolio as roles that especially interested him. In 'Turtlenecks' Curtis played a middle-aged man who writes half-time shows in America for release during the breaks in football matches. The play flopped, not even reaching Broadway. "It was very disappointing", Curtis said afterwards. "Everything turned out to be wrong with it. I went into it with all the vitality, drive and energy at my command. Then you find you have made a mistake, another mistake and you get your head handed back to you on a plate again. I felt very alone, despondent and in the middle of a vortex at that time. I had an option to get out at Philadelphia so I did. I had to nurse my wounds after that play. It was a very tough time. I was a basket case by the end but there is nothing you can do. It is the nature of the profession."

Then, in 1974 the man who had said 'never again' was back making movies, his enthusiasm apparently rekindled. Questioned about his comeback he replied; "Well, I guess it is the nature of film-making that you never lose interest altogether. You just want to make movies. It was inevitable. Showbusiness is the toughest rat race there is. Now I'm more selective but it is always on my terms". The film that tempted him back was 'Lepke', a pacy biography of Jewish mobster Louis Lepke that provided him with one of his best latter-day roles and sparked a strong dramatic turn from Curtis. The film was greeted with acclaim at the Cannes Film Festival of 1974 and a more mixed response elsewhere. "The response at Cannes was so stimulating. You spend years searching for a way to express yourself in films and there are not many that you find. When you do it is very exciting. I was intrigued by this man as I was about Albert De Salvo. Here was a man, Jewish Brooklyn-born who had two hundred killers on contract to him all making ten to one hundred thousand dollars a year from their business. I wanted to know what was in his background, his environment, that made him that kind of man. You know he was the only one of the kingpin gangsters of that era who died in the electric chair. He was so powerful none of the other guys tried to bump him off. He made Capone and the others look like chopped liver."

Curtis's second comeback film was a swashbuckler, 'The Count of Monte Cristo', and it was suggested that in some way his career had come full circle. "I seem to be interested in period films but am I a back where I started? Yeah, perhaps I am. I had thought about it. But please God I don't have to go through it ALL again. I don't think so."

The last decade has not been the happiest for Curtis either personally or professionally. In November 1974 he was scheduled to begin work in Rome on 'The Man in the Iron Mask', the film was cancelled and led to litigation over his fee. In 1975 he made a television series in America called 'McCoy' which was one of a rotating series of Mystery Movies that included 'McCloud', 'Columbo' and 'McMillan and Wife'. Curtis's series flopped and lasted only four episodes. In 1976 he was supposed to begin work on a unnamed project for producer Freddie Fields and Paramount in Hollywood, it was not made. However the 'Seventies were not a period of unrelieved professional gloom and Curtis remained as enthusiastic and positive as ever. In 1975 he said; "I've been through ups and downs and here I am —internationally known all over the place. Isn't that thrilling? Isn't it wonderful to think I've got that going?". A few years later, when he had completed one of his few comic roles of recent times in 'The Bad News Bears Go To

With Janet Leigh receiving an award as the most co-operative stars

Japan' he told The Hollywood Reporter; "I like my work in films, and I like writing and painting but what's most important to me is living. I take care of myself to enjoy life. You can't live well without being healthy. I eat simply. . . fresh orange juice with two raw eggs in the morning, never any lunch, maybe an apple in the afternoon, and in the evening my dear wife will fix, say, chicken with rice and a big salad, and I'm happy. What keeps me fit is an active sex life. I'm horny. I have no hang-ups about it. Also, art comes out of sexuality (doesn't everything?) it's another form of ejaculation, peak, renewal. Nothing can beat rubbing against someone's leg and boom. . . a thousand colours flash." He was happily still with Leslie and, as with his previous marriages, he ensured that his wife was involved in his work and Leslie was prevailed upon to appear in 'The Last Tycoon' and in one of the 'McCoy' episodes. In F. Scott Fitzgerald's 'The Last Tycoon' (1976) he had given a carefully etched portrait of a movie idol worried by age, fading looks and impotence. It seemed to presage a new career as a character actor but, instead led nowhere, and in later years gossip columnists would suggest that life was eerily mirroring Fitzgerald's fiction for Curtis.

His recent films are, by and large, a sorry bunch best passed over in discreet silence. He has been desperately unlucky in his choice of material. The only compensating successes have been on television where he had a recurring role in the popular series 'Vegas' and was nominated for an Emmy, television's equivalent of the Oscar, for his spirited portrayal of movie tycoon David O. Selznick in 'The Scarlett O'Hara War' segment of Garson Kanin's 'Moviola'.

The Year 1980 promised much for Curtis, it looked on paper like another chance for him to pull everything together. On television he had Moviola in prospect, for the cinema he had a supporting role in a potential hit film, 'Little Miss Marker', and he received an interesting stage offer — the lead role in a play by Neil Simon, surely the most consistently commercial writer in the post-war American theatre. He also intended to concentrate more time on his two youngest children, Nicholas and Benjamin, and his twelve-year marriage to Leslie which was showing signs of strain. In 1979, when the couple had temporarily separated, Curtis moved out of their house and took up residence in the mansion of his friend Hugh Hefner.

Simon's play, 'I Ought To Be In Pictures', is about a young girl's quest to re-establish relations with her father, a Hollywood screen-writer who is not as successful as his estranged family had believed. She heads for California and an instant antipathy between father and daughter is broken down resulting in reconciliation. Simon had offered the part to Walter Matthau who, unofficially retired from the stage, declined the role. Simon settled for Curtis and the play began its run in Los Angeles prior to opening in New York. The play was poorly received although Curtis himself was better liked. It was announced that Curtis would not be taking the play to Broadway and that Ron Leibman would take over in his place. Then, during one performance Curtis did not return for the second act after the interval. The audience were informed that he was unable to continue owing to illness. He did not return for the remainder of the Los Angeles run. Speculation was rife as to the reason behind his conduct. It was claimed that he was furious about his replacement rehearsing with the cast every afternoon, that he did not get on with the director Herbert Ross, and that he resented that Simon was writing a new first act to improve the play while Curtis was abandoned to the old script. Later in the year Curtis told his side of the story; "I had such a terrible time with these two gentlemen. I thought I'd be in the company of quality people. I was wrong. Neil Simon's behaviour towards me was shoddy. And Herb Ross gave me no help at all. When Neil Simon began to rewrite the first act, I knew it was impossible to go on. I tell you — I was so pleased when I heard I didn't have to go to New York. But you know how I heard? From the stage manager. Those two gentlemen didn't have the class to sit down and say: 'Listen Tony we think its better if you don't take it to Broadway'. I never saw them after that. It's just as well. In the worst movie I ever made I wasn't treated as badly as I was during the times I was with that play. Worst of all were the rumours spread about my departure. People began saying that I was on drugs. That's criminal man, saying a thing like that."

In March 1980 'Little Miss Marker' was released and proved not to be as popular as anticipated. To make matters worse for Curtis his long marriage to Leslie was deteriorating and the couple split for good. The accumulation of worries and setbacks were too much for Curtis and he secretly checked into a clinic in Pasadena. A fellow patient was reported as saying; "When he arrived he was a shambling wreck. He looked hunted and haunted. His face was grey and he seemed old". Rumours abounded that he was tormented by growing old, his fading sex appeal and his third divorce. It was claimed that Leslie lived in constant fear of him and that he had threatened her life. From all the press speculation he appeared to have reached the depths of despair. Yet, within a few months 'Moviola' had appeared on television, garnering him an excellent set of personal reviews, and by the summertime he was back at work making a film in Britain: 'The Mirror Crack'd'. That film's director, Guy Hamilton, noticed how Curtis went out of his way to help his co-stars, particularly Rock Hudson a worrier at the beginning of any film assignment. Hamilton stated; "Tony Curtis I noticed held Rock Hudson's arm as often as possible in their early scenes together. Hudson needed the re-assurance of physical contact". Questioned as to the enduring appeal of the 'Fifties stars featured in the film Curtis chuckled; "People will come to see how we have all aged." These minor incidents hardly paint a picture of a frightened, suicidal movie idol worried that he was all washed up.

Later in 1980 Curtis talked about his traumatic year; "I'll be honest with you", he told Sunday Express writer Roderick Mann. "It's been a bad time: a bitch of a time. But I'm all right now." Discussing the break-up of his longest lasting marriage he said; "Her rejection damaged my ego so badly that I used to sleep in the back of my car. It seemed better than going indoors to face the reality of our deteriorating relationship. Fighting to keep my marriage together, then struggling to keep my misery and despair in check were too much. I was admitted to hospital. The doctors said I had severe melancholia. My depression was so deep I just couldn't cope with it anymore. I did not turn to drink or drugs for comfort although it might have been understandable if I had. I was living through a mental turmoil as I saw my life being ripped to shreds. But it's behind me now. It goes without saying that I miss my wife Leslie and my family. But I've got a place of my own now in Bel Air and I'm gradually getting used to living alone. I used to be scared of the prospect but not anymore." During a visit to London he summed up his year when he noted; "I survived. I didn't turn to drink or drugs, nothing like that. As a matter of fact I've given up everything. If I find I can't sleep now I just call down to room service and they send me up some warm milk. I'm going to be all right. Really."

At the time of his troubles friends rallied and a lavish party was given in his honour by producer Allan Carr attended by Kirk Douglas, Hugh Hefner, Jaclyn Smith, Tina Sinatra, Peter Falk and many more. He was never short of female company to help share his sorrows and his name was linked with former Charlie's Angel Jaclyn Smith and Soraya Khashoggi the former wife of an Arabian billionaire. He kept busy working for television and making the occasional film though, given the generally poor quality of the material offered, one wonders why he has bothered. He certainly didn't need the money having invested his earnings wisely in such things as California real estate. Everywhere he travels he carries a piece of paper detailing his worth and was quoted as saying; "I know exactly what I'm worth wherever I am. I'm not a spendthrift, I'm not going to go down the tubes broke." Perhaps the explanation for making films like 'Othello — The Black Commando' is the need to keep busy and fill the time in which one might otherwise brood and despair.

In the last few years his name has appeared in the more sensationalistic tabloid newspapers which highlight his sad decline with gossip about depressions, drug-addiction, alcoholism and illnesses. How much truth lies behind the headlines is hard to ascertain. In 1982 Christine Kaufmann published nude photos of their sixteen year old daughter Alexandra. She claimed: "I want to make Tony Curtis mad at me because of these photographs. I want to show him how beautiful his daughter has become." Kaufmann also revealed that she had taken her daughters from Curtis two years previously because they had asked to be set free from their 'drinking, drug-taking' father. Curtis replied that he was well aware how beautiful his daughter had become and dismissed Kaufmann's actions as a cheap trick to make a fast buck. He again denied being a drug-addict.

In 1983 there was an announcement that he might retire to Switzerland and open an art gallery, a wise move it seemed. However, there was also speculation that Curtis's friend Allan Carr planned to team Curtis and Jack Lemmon in his Broadway production 'La Cage Aux Folles'. Curtis's daughter Jamie Lee was now probably a better known star to the younger filmgoing generation than her father. For a while she had appeared to have become typecast as the queen of the screamers in low-budget films like 'Halloween' (1978), 'The Fog' (1979) which co-starred Janet Leigh, and 'Terror Train' (1980). Through a determined effort to broaden her range she was cast in the wildly successful comedy 'Trading Places' (1983) and won a British Academy Award as Best Supporting Actress.

Curtis, looking quite his jaunty old self, breezed through Heathrow airport in the summer of 1983 hand in hand with young actress Andria Savio claiming that the couple hoped to be married soon. Within a few months he was back in Britain, and back in the film-making business appearing opposite Orson Welles in the comedy 'Where Is Parsifal?'.

During the spring and summer of 1984 Curtis's name was rarely absent from newspaper headlines. As so often in recent times it was for all the wrong reasons. In April he collapsed at his Bel Air home and was rushed to the Cedars Sinai Medical Centre. His condition was diagnosed as severe cirrhosis of the liver and internal bleeding. Shortly afterwards he registered at the Betty Ford Centre at Rancho Mirage in California. The Centre is a Clinic specialising in drug and drink related problems and has recently played host to an alarming number of showbusiness celebrities including Elizabeth Taylor and Johnny Cash. According to press reports Curtis had stated that this was a 'last ditch' attempt to beat serious drug and alcohol problems and had told friends; "it's now or never." One friend was quoted as saying; "He cannot stand being a former screen idol. He's a very sick man."

The treatment appears to have been successful and Curtis was discharged after a three week hospitalization. At a twenty-fifth anniversary celebration for 'Some Like It Hot' he announced that, prior to entering the Betty Ford Centre, he had secretly wed Andria Savio, 22, his girlfriend of three years. He was quoted as saying; "Andria has helped me through all my problems. We want to have a family as soon as possible. I am now going to AA meetings and I am determined to lick my problem. I can talk publicly about my problems now because I want to help others."

It seemed like another happy ending for Tony Curtis but regular followers of his life might have known that nothing is ever that straightforward for this man. Five weeks after the marriage announcement Miss Savio told the press that it had all been a hoax engineered to aid Curtis's career. She was quoted in one interview saying; "I helped him get over drugs and he turned into a creaky, complaining old man. He wanted to resume his career and part of the process was saying that he was married. He thought it gave him an image of stability. He wanted himself to look good." Savio had now left Curtis and, it was asserted, was considering suing the actor for 'palimony' —the term that has come to

Meeting James Stewart on his arrival in Hollywood in 1948

signify a form of alimony among Hollywood's unmarried couples. The Tony Curtis story, it appears, will continue to remain as dramatic as ever.

An an actor Tony Curtis improved from a green youngster tripping over his thick Bronx vowels into an accomplished and versatile performer. His craft is important to him and, although he always wanted to be a star and played that role to the hilt, he was equally diligent as an actor of merit. Part of his style is to conquer a role with his dynamism and energy. Writing in 'The Times' in 1971 Michael Billington observed; "Curtis's own approach to acting might well be described as Olympic. After the first rehearsal of a scene he will ask the continuity girl how long it lasts; if she says fifty seconds he will try and get it down in time to thirty-eight. Apart from pace he also believes in research." Curtis himself has explained; "Acting to me is very much like making love. It's something very personal and private and I don't like people sharing it with me. I want them to see the finished product. I don't want them to see me fighting and struggling for those moments of truth."

In recent years he has appeared in largely poor scripts from mainly second rate directors and his reputation and career have suffered as a consequence. His desire to break away from working within the major studios and assert his independence as a freelance worker, his sabbatical in Britain and announcement of retiral, combined with personal and health problems, have added up to a career of fewer offers and certainly fewer good offers. Yet, in the right circumstances, notably 'Moviola' in 1980, he can be as effective and winning as ever.

Tony Curtis the man is a creature of many passions; an actor, a painter, an art collector and a writer. He once said; "Writing isn't a sideline with me. Nothing is a sideline". He has been a long-standing anti-smoking campaigner and health food advocate. In America he appeared in nationwide commercials to promote an I.Q. (I Quit) anti-smoking drive. The commercials were dropped when he was arrested at an airport charged with possession of marijuana. He is also a devoted connoisseur of women and has said; "I had the rare opportunity of being famous at an early age, with a little money in my pocket, and I was able to feast myself on women in every environment I was in. Sex takes on different moods in other locales". He then proceeded to give a gourmet's guide to the women of the world. One can only assume that his roving eye has contributed to the break up of his three marriages, alongside his often compulsive submersion in the current standing of his career and a fairly sizeable ego.

Curtis the man seems a strange balance of charm, good-humour and healthy ambition on the one hand and paranoia, insecurity and superstition on the other. Interviewers have noted his warmth and sincerity, and colleagues like Sidney Poitier have testified to the generosity of his spirit. In his autobiography 'This Life,' Poitier commented; "I met Tony Curtis, and he was terrific. His very first kindness to me was when he said to Stanley Kramer, 'Listen, I don't want to be on the top of the picture by myself. Why don't you but Poitier up there with me?'. He insisted that I be given co-star billing for the first time in my career, saying, 'What is this? Put him up there too!' And in those days getting co-star billing above the title was difficult". Yet, others have found him brash and aggressive. When his career and private life are in harmony he seems at peace, a happy family man, when things are otherwise he seems prone to an embittered and consuming paranoia, unable to reconcile himself to changing times. He once asked; "Where is there a weakness in me? What do I do that can make a woman so frustrated and angry that she can't live with me? That's my problem. I don't know whether everything I've done makes complete sense — or the way I've gone about it. We are all human beings and we have go to be what we are. We can't pretend and we've got to make our own mistakes."

In 1965 he offered a harsh self-judgement; "In the history of things movie-wise I'll probably rate a three line entry as the character who gave a hairstyle to the Teddyboys of the 'Fifties." The gifted star of films like 'Sweet Smell of Success', 'The Defiant Ones', 'Some Like It Hot', 'The Outsider' and 'The Boston Strangler' deserves better.

In June of 1984 Curtis was announced as the star of two new films; 'King of the City' and 'Insignificance'. The former will be produced and directed by Norman Thaddeus Vane and co-stars Stella Stevens and Michael Parks. Curtis will be joined in 'Insignificance' by Theresa Russell, Gary Busey, Michael Emil and Will Sampson. The film's producer is Jeremy Thomas and the director the highly talented Nicolas Roeg whose previous films include 'Don't Look Now', 'The Man Who Fell to Earth', 'Bad Timing' and 'Eureka'. It would appear that Tony Curtis, the survivor, is back in business.

THE MOVIES

1949: Criss Cross
City Across the River
The Lady Gambles
Johnny Stool Pigeon
1950: Francis
I Was a Shoplifter
Winchester 73
Sierra
Kansas Raiders
1951: The Prince Who Was A Thief
1952: Son of Ali Baba
Flesh and Fury
No Room for the Groom
1953: Houdini
The All American
Forbidden
1954: Beachhead
Johnny Dark
The Black Shield of Falworth
So This Is Paris
Six Bridges To Cross
1955: The Purple Mask
The Square Jungle
The Rawhide Years
1956: Trapeze
Mister Cory
1957: The Midnight Story
Sweet Smell Of Success
1958: The Vikings
The Defiant Ones
Kings Go Forth
The Perfect Furlough
1959: Some Like It Hot
Operation Petticoat
Who Was That Lady?
1960: The Rat Race
Spartacus
The Great Imposter
1961: The Outsider
1962: Taras Bulba
Forty Pounds of Trouble
1963: Captain Newman M.D.

1964: Wild and Wonderful
Goodbye Charlie
Sex and the Single Girl
1965: The Great Race
Boeing, Boeing
1966: Not With My Wife You Don't
Drop Dead Darling
1967: Don't Make Waves
The Chastity Belt
1968: The Boston Strangler
1969: Monte Carlo Or Bust!
Suppose They Gave A War
And Nobody Came
1970: You Can't Win 'Em All
1974: Lepke
The Count of Monte Cristo
1976: The Last Tycoon
1977: Casanova and Co.
The Manitou
Sextette
1978: The Bad News Bears Go
To Japan
1979: It Rained All Night The Day I
Left
Title Shot
1980: Little Miss Marker
The Mirror Crack'd
1982: Brainwaves
Othello - The Black
Commando
Balbao
1984: Where Is Parsifal?

Others:
1960: Pepe (guest)
1963: The List of Adrian Messenger
(guest)
1964: Paris When It Sizzles (guest)
1966: Chamber of Horrors (guest)
1968: Rosemary's Baby
(voice only)

THE APPRENTICESHIP

In the immediate post-war years Universal talent scouts signed many promising youngsters to a standard seven-year contract on their services. The youngsters would go through a form of training at the various departments at Universal International Studios in California. They would take lessons in deportment, drama, voice command, fencing, horse riding and all the skills thought necessary to further their screen careers. Then they were allowed to actually make films, generally starting with small roles in the more prestigious Universal features, and with more substantial opportunities to be found in the studio's second features or in on-going series like the 'Francis the Talking Mule' films or the latest escapades of 'Ma and Pa Kettle'. When Bernard Schwartz arrived at Universal in 1948 the biggest stars at the studio were probably Deanna Durbin and the comedy duo of Abbott and Costello.

Renamed Anthony Curtis he made his film debut in 'Criss Cross', released in 1949. He appears in just a few moments of film, dancing with the leading lady Yvonne De Carlo. The reaction to his appearance so overwhelmed the studio that he was quickly employed in several features. 'City Across the River' (1949) told the story of 'The Dukes' a gang of young hoods from the Brooklyn slums. Based on a novel by Irving Shulman the film allowed Universal to employ several of the young contract players as gang members. Aside from Curtis the others included Richard Jaeckel, Al Ramsen, Joshua Shelley and Mickey Knox. The film claimed to have been made on the streets of Brooklyn and was one of a number of films in a drama-documentary format dealing with juvenile delinquency. The Sunday Pictorial of 1949 thought that; "This film unearths some very promising young talent and really does bring to life most of the unpleasant aspects of a slum community."

'The Lady Gambles' (1949) used a strong line up of acting talent with a cast headed by Barbara Stanwyck, Robert Preston and Stephen McNally. Stanwyck plays a money-squandering wife addicted to gambling who abandons her husband to pursue her compulsion. Poverty-stricken and involved with some unsavoury characters she attempts suicide but is tracked down by her loyal husband and the couple are reconciled. Curtis plays a hotel bellboy. He had a much more telling role in 'Johnny Stool Pigeon' (1949) (also known as 'Partners in Crime') as deaf mute killer Joe Hyatt involved in the drugs ring of Nick Avery (John McIntire) which is eventually uncovered by Treasury Department Narcotics agents led by Howard Duff's George Morton. Reviewing the film the Monthly Film Bulletin thought; "The story has too many contrivances; but there is some good characterisation and its forceful method of approach effectively sustains tension. It is excellently acted."

In 1950 Curtis was seen in roles of varying importance in five releases. In 'Francis' he had little to do as an army member among the many men in the troop of one Peter Stirling (Donald O'Connor) who has an on-going friendship with a talking mule called Francis. The film had its premiere before an audience of GIs in Berlin which Donald O'Connor attended at the invitation of the American Air Force. In America the film was one of Universal's biggest hits of the year, taking some three million dollars. A series followed starring O'Connor and the mule whose voice was provided by Chill Wills. The titles were 'Francis Goes to the Races' (1951) with Piper Laurie, 'Francis Goes to West Point' (1952) with Lori Nelson, 'Francis Covers the Big Town' (1953) with Nancy Guild, 'Francis joins the Wacs' (1954) with Julia Adams and 'Francis in the Navy' (1955) with Martha Hyer and a young Clint Eastwood. O'Connor then left the series explaining; "When you've made six pictures and the the mule still gets more fan mail than you do...". One further adventure followed — 'Francis in the Haunted House' (1956) with Mickey Rooney and Virginia Welles.

The deluge of fan mail for Anthony Curtis conveyed to the studio the strength of public feeling about the young star and they began entrusting him with some better roles. In 'I was a Shoplifter' he was fourth-billed as thug Pepe in a story about an undercover expose of a shoplifting ring. The Universal publicity department hailed the film as— "a timely exposure of this growing social menace in America." Curtis's other 1950 releases were all Westerns. Two, 'Sierra' and 'Kansas Raiders', starred Audie Murphy. In the latter Curtis played the true life character of Kit Dalton who joins with Murphy's Jessie James to ride in Quantrill's Raiders. The most enduring of his 1950 films has been 'Winchester '73', a

The Kobal Collection

classic Western starring James Stewart as a vengeance-seeking brother. Remade in 1967 the episodic story is built around the various adventures that befall the owners of a "Winchester '73 repeating rifle which Stewart wins in a competition but subsequently has stolen from his possession. Curtis has a few lines of dialogue as cavalry trooper Doan and Rock Hudson makes an early appearance as Indian leader Young Bull. The film was much praised on its release with this Sunday Times review giving a representative view; Winchester '73 has the pace and the sweep, the crisp dialogue and the equally crisp black and white image to permit it to act as a yardstick for the other horse-operas." The film was a notable success and began Stewart's fruitful collaboration with director Anthony Mann which later produced a further seven films including; 'The Naked Spur' (1953), 'The Glenn Miller Story' (1953) and 'The Man from Laramie' (1955).

In his early film roles Curtis was given an opportunity to gain experience in working for the medium of cinema. The roles assigned to him were not meant to stretch him as an actor but to establish him as a screen presence. The studio wisely, in view of his pronounced Bronx accent and inexperience, restricted him to roles within these limitations — a bellboy, a trooper, a thug or a juvenile delinquent from the streets of New York. His growing popularity, reflected in his fan mail, led the studio to gamble on him as star material and thus he was singled out from other contract hopefuls to play the leading role in 'The Prince Who Was A Thief'. The rest, as they say, is history.

CRISS CROSS

U.S.A. 1949 – RUNNING TIME: 87 MINUTES
UNIVERSAL-INTERNATIONAL

		CAST	
DIRECTOR:	ROBERT SIODMAK		
PRODUCER:	MICHAEL KRAIKE		
SCREENPLAY:	DANIEL FUCHS FROM THE NOVEL BY	BURT LANCASTER:	STEVE THOMPSON
	DON TRACY	YVONNE DE CARLO:	ANNA
ART DIRECTION:	BERNARD HERZBRUN AND BORIS LEVEN	DAN DURYEA:	SLIM DUNDEE
DIRECTOR OF PHOTOGRAPHY:	FRANZ PLANER	STEPHEN MCNALLY:	PETE RAMIREZ
EDITOR:	TED J. KENT	RICHARD LONG:	SLADE THOMPSON
SOUND:	LESLIE I. CAREY AND RICHARD DE WEESE	MEG RANDELL:	HELEN
MUSIC	MIKLOS ROZSA	ESY MORALES:	ORCHESTRA LEADER
COSTUMES:	YVONNE WOOD	TOM PEDI:	VINCENT
		PERCY HELTON:	FRANK
		ALAN NAPIER:	FINCHLEY
		GRIFF BARNETT:	POP
		EDNA M. HOLLAND:	MRS THOMPSON
		ANTHONY CURTIS:	GIGOLO

CITY ACROSS THE RIVER

U.S.A. 1949 – RUNNING TIME: 91 MINUTES
UNIVERSAL-INTERNATIONAL

		CAST	
DIRECTOR:	MAXWELL SHANE		
PRODUCER:	MAXWELL SHANE		
ASSOCIATE PRODUCER:	BEN COLMAN	STEPHEN MCNALLY	STAN ALBERT
SCREENPLAY:	MAXWELL SHANE AND DENNIS COOPER	THELMA RITTER	MRS CUSACK
	FROM THE NOVEL 'THE AMBOY DUKES'	LUIS VAN ROOTEN	JOE CUSACK
	BY IRVING SHULMAN	JEFF COREY	LT. MACON
ART DIRECTION:	BERNARD HERZBRUN AND	SHARON MCMANUS	ALICE CUSACK
	EMRICH NICHOLSON	SUE ENGLAND	BETTY
DIRECTOR OF PHOTOGRAPHY:	MAURY GERTSMAN	BARBARA WHITING	ANNIE KANE
EDITOR:	TED J. KENT	RICHARD BENEDICT	GAGGSY STEENS
SOUND:	LESLIE I. CAREY AND JOE LAPIS	ANABEL SHAW	JEAN ALBERT
MUSIC:	WALTER SCHARF	ANTHONY CURTIS	MITCH
		RICHARD JAECKEL	BULL

THE LADY GAMBLES

U.S.A. 1949 – RUNNING TIME: 99 MINUTES
UNIVERSAL-INTERNATIONAL

		CAST	
DIRECTOR:	MICHAEL GORDON		
PRODUCER:	MICHAEL KRAIKE		
SCREENPLAY:	ROY HUGGINS, ADAPTED BY HALSTEAD	BARBARA STANWYCK	JOAN BOOTHE
	WELLS FROM A STORY BY LEWIS MELTZER	ROBERT PRESTON	DAVID BOOTHE
	AND OSCAR SAUL	STEPHEN MCNALLY	CORRIGAN
ART DIRECTION:	ALEXANDER GOLITZEN	EDITH BARRETT	RUTH PHILLIPS
DIRECTOR OF PHOTOGRAPHY:	RUSSEL METTY	JOHN HOYT	DR ROJAC
EDITOR:	MILTON CARRUTH	ELLIOTT SULLIVAN	BARKY
MUSIC:	FRANK SKINNER	JOHN HARMON	FRENCHY
COSTUMES:	ORRY KELLY	LEIF ERICKSON	TONY
		CURT CONWAY	BANK CLERK
		DON BEDDOE	MR SUTHERLAND
		NANA BRYANT	MRS SUTHERLAND
		ANTHONY CURTIS	BELLBOY

JOHNNY STOOL PIDGEON

A.K.A. PARTNERS IN CRIME
U.S.A. 1949 – RUNNING TIME: 75 MINUTES
UNIVERSAL-INTERNATIONAL

DIRECTOR:	WILLIAM CASTLE
PRODUCER:	AARON ROSENBERG
SCREENPLAY:	ROBERT L RICHARDS FROM A STORY
	BY HENRY JORDAN
ART DIRECTION:	EMRICH NICHOLSON AND
	BERNARD HERZBRUN
DIRECTOR OF PHOTOGRAPHY:	MAURY GERTSMAN
EDITOR:	TED KENT
SOUND:	LESLIE CAREY AND RICHARD DE WEESE
PRODUCTION MANAGER:	DEWEY STARKEY
MUSIC:	MILTON SCHWARZWALD
COSTUMES	ORRY KELLY

CAST

HOWARD DUFF	GEORGE MORTON
SHELLEY WINTERS	TERRY
DAN DURYEA	JOHNNY EVANS
TONY CURTIS	JOEY HYATT
JOHN MCINTIRE	NICK AVERY
GAR MOORE	SAM HARRISON
LEIF ERICKSON	PRINGLE
BARRY KELLEY	MCCANDLES
HUGH REILLY	CHARLIE
WALLY MAHER	BENSON
NACHO GALINDO	MARTINEZ

FRANCIS

U.S.A. 1950 – RUNNING TIME: 90 MINUTES
UNIVERSAL-INTERNATIONAL

DIRECTOR:	ARTHUR LUBIN
PRODUCER:	ROBERT ARTHUR
SCREENPLAY:	DAVID STERN FROM HIS OWN NOVEL
ART DIRECTION:	BERNARD HERZBRUN AND
	RICHARD H. RIEDEL
DIRECTOR OF PHOTOGRAPHY:	IRVING GLASSBERG
EDITOR:	MILTON CARRUTH
SOUND:	LESLIE I CAREY AND CORSON JOWETT
MUSIC:	FRANK SKINNER
COSTUMES:	ROSEMARY ODELL

CAST

DONALD O'CONNOR	PETER STIRLING
PATRICIA MEDINA	MAUREEN GELDER
ZASU PITTS	VALERIE HUMPERT
RAY COLLINS	COL. HOOKER
JOHN MCINTIRE	GENERAL STEVENS
EDUARD FRANZ	COL. PLEPPER
JAMES TODD	COL. SAUNDERS
ROBERT WARWICK	COL. CARMICHAEL
FRANK FAYLEN	SGT. CHILLINGBACKER
ANTHONY CURTIS	CAPT. JONES

I WAS A SHOPLIFTER

U.S.A. 1950 – RUNNING TIME: 82 MINUTES
UNIVERSAL-INTERNATIONAL

DIRECTOR:	CHARLES LAMONT
PRODUCER:	LEONARD GOLDSTEIN
SCREENPLAY:	IRWIN GIELGUD
ART DIRECTION:	BERNARD HERZBRUN AND
	ROBERT CLATWORTHY
DIRECTOR OF PHOTOGRAPHY:	IRVING GLASSBERG
EDITOR:	OTTO LUDWIG
SOUND:	LESLIE I. CAREY AND ROBERT PRITCHARD
MUSIC:	MILTON SCHWARZWALD
COSTUMES:	ROSEMARY ODELL

CAST

SCOTT BRADY	JEFF ANDREWS
MONA FREEMAN	FAYE BURTON
ANDREA KING	INA PERDUE
ANTHONY CURTIS	PEPE
CHARLES DRAKE	HERB KLAXTON
GREGG MARTELL	THE CHAMP
ROBERT GIST	BARKIE NEFF
LARRY KEATING	HARRY DUNSON
MICHAEL RAFFETTO	SHERIFF BASCON
CHARLES MCGRAW	MAN
ROCK HUDSON	STORE DETECTIVE

The Kobal Collection

WINCHESTER '73

U.S.A. 1950 – RUNNING TIME: 92 MINUTES
UNIVERSAL-INTERNATIONAL

		CAST	
DIRECTOR:	ANTHONY MANN		
PRODUCER:	AARON ROSENBERG		
SCREENPLAY:	ROBERT L. RICHARDS AND BORDEN CHASE	JAMES STEWART	LIN MCADAM
	FROM A STORY BY STUART N. LAKE	SHELLEY WINTERS	LOLA MANNERS
ART DIRECTION:	BERNARD HERZBRUN AND	DAN DURYEA	WACO JOHNNY DEAN
	NATHAN JURAN	STEPHEN MCNALLY	DUTCH HENRY BROWN
DIRECTOR OF PHOTOGRAPHY:	WILLIAM DANIELS	MILLARD MITCHELL	JOHNNY WILLIAMS
EDITOR:	EDWARD CURTISS	CHARLES DRAKE	STEVE MILLER
SOUND:	LESLIE I. CAREY AND RICHARD DE WEESE	JOHN MCINTIRE	JOE LAMONT
MUSIC:	JOSEPH GERSHENSON	WILL GEER	WYATT EARP
COSTUMES:	YVONNE WOOD	JAY C. FLIPPEN	SGT. WILKES
		ROCK HUDSON	YOUNG BULL
		TONY CURTIS	DOAN

SIERRA

U.S.A. 1950 – RUNNING TIME: 83 MINUTES
UNIVERSAL-INTERNATIONAL

		CAST	
DIRECTOR:	ALFRED E GREEN		
PRODUCER:	MICHAEL KRAIKE		
SCREENPLAY:	EDNA ANHALT FROM A NOVEL BY	WANDA HENDRIX	RILEY MARTIN
	STUART HARDY	AUDIE MURPHY	RING HASSARD
ART DIRECTION:	BERNARD HERZBRUN AND	BURL IVES	LONESOME
	ROBERT F. BOYLE	DEAN JAGGER	JEFF HASSARD
DIRECTOR OF PHOTOGRAPHY:	RUSSELL METTY	RICHARD ROBER	BIG MATI
EDITOR:	TED J. KENT	TONY CURTIS	BRENT COULTER
SOUND:	LESLIE I. CAREY AND GLENN E. ANDERSON	HOUSELEY STEVENSON	SAM COULTER
MUSIC:	WALTER SCHARF	ELLIOT REID	DUKE LAFFERTY

KANSAS RAIDERS

U.S.A. 1950 – RUNNING TIME: 80 MINUTES
UNIVERSAL-INTERNATIONAL

		CAST	
DIRECTOR:	RAY ENRIGHT		
PRODUCER:	TED RICHMOND		
SCREENPLAY:	ROBERT L. RICHARDS	AUDIE MURPHY	JESSE JAMES
ART DIRECTION:	BERNARD HERZBRUN AND	BRIAN DONLEVY	QUANTRILL
	EMRICH NICHOLSON	MARGUERITE CHAPMAN	KATE CLARKE
DIRECTOR OF PHOTOGRAPHY:	IRVING GLASSBERG	SCOTT BRADY	BILL ANDERSON
EDITOR:	MILTON CARRUTH	TONY CURTIS	KIT DALTON
MUSIC:	JOSEPH GERSHENSON	RICHARD ARLEN	UNION CAPTAIN
		RICHARD LONG	FRANK JAMES
		JAMES BEST	COLE YOUNGER
		JOHN KELLOGG	RED LEG LEADER
		DEWEY MARTIN	JAMES YOUNGER

THE PRINCE WHO WAS A THIEF

U.S.A. 1951 – RUNNING TIME: 88 MINUTES
UNIVERSAL-INTERNATIONAL

		CAST	
DIRECTOR:	RUDOLPH MATÉ		
PRODUCER:	LEONARD GOLDSTEIN		
SCREENPLAY:	GERALD DRAYSON ADAMS AND	TONY CURTIS	JULNA
AENEAS MACKENZIE FROM A STORY BY THEODORE DREISER		PIPER LAURIE	TINA
ART DIRECTION:	BERNARD HERZBRUN AND	EVERETT SLOANE	YUSSEF
	EMRICH NICHOLSON	JEFF COREY	MOKAR
DIRECTOR OF PHOTOGRAPHY:	IRVING GLASSBERG	BETTY GARDE	MIRZA
EDITOR:	EDWARD CURTISS	MARVIN MILLER	HAKAR
SOUND:	LESLIE I. CAREY AND GLENN ANDERSON	PEGGIE CASTLE	PRINCESS YASHIM
MUSIC:	HANS SALTER	DONALD RANDOLPH	MUSTAPHA
COSTUMES:	BILL THOMAS	NITA BIEBER	CAHUENA
		MILADA MLADOVA	DANCER
		HAYDEN RORKE	BASRA
		MIDGE WARE	SARI
		CAROL VARGA	BEULAH

Like Curtis, Piper Laurie was a young Universal contract player. Born Rosetta Jacobs in Detroit she had later moved to Los Angeles, taken an interest in acting and been spotted by a Universal talent scout. Signed to a long-term contract she joined Universal aged just 17. In her second year at the studio she was chosen as Curtis's partner for what was viewed as an inexpensive Arabian Knights programmer. Unexpectedly the film's mixture of colourful escapism and energetic high jinks made it a considerable box-office success. Virtually overnight Curtis and Laurie were hailed as teenage idols, the fan mail poured in and Universal found itself with a potent screen team.

The basis for the film was a short story by the accomplished American novelist Theodore Dreiser whose more notable books included 'An American Tragedy' and 'Carrie'.

Prince Mustapha hires the thief Yussef to slay the princeling Hussein, heir to the throne of the House of Marshan. Yussef is unable to complete the task and, instead, smuggles the child into the protective care of his home, raising him as his own son. The only sign of Hussein's real identity is a gold falcon tattoo mark.

Nineteen years later Hussein has grown into a master thief under the assumed name of Julna. Julna meets his match in fellow thief Tina who steals the Pink Pearl of Fatima from the chambers of Princess Yanee, the daughter of Prince Mustapha. Yussef is accused of the theft and ordered to return the pearl or forfeit his life. Julna manages to trick Tina into returning the pearl which she then proceeds to steal again.

When Julna is beaten for an offence committed by Tina she is reluctantly obliged to give him the pearl to return to the Princess (who has offered her hand in marriage to the one who returns the jewel). During an argument Julna has revealed to Tina that he is Prince Hussein so she begs him to beware of the Princess's motives. Julna disregards this advice and, upon entering the Palace, is captured by guards. During the ensuing skirmish Julna escapes but Tina is held captive. With the aid of bandit leader Zocco and the Jackals, Julna and Yussef raid the Palace. They are taken prisoner, but when Julna reveals that he is Prince Hussein the troops acknowledge him as their leader and Mustapha is discredited. Princess Yanee tries to kill Julna but is prevented from doing so by Tina. All ends happily as Julna and Tina are married.

Universal-International

"Curtis, in a dashing portrayal that brings back fond memories of Douglas Fairbanks and Rudolph Valentino certainly establishes himself as moviedom's most exciting newcomer in this film. Combining a handsome face and figure with both athletic prowess and true skill as an actor, he brings to life the title role with amazing dexterity."

SCREEN PARADE

"The movie is energetically played, well-paced by director Rudolph Maté, occasionally touched with humour and quite free of pretensions. It should delight youngsters without irritating the grown-ups who go along for the air condition."

TIME

SON OF ALI BABA

U.S.A. 1952 – RUNNING TIME: 75 MINUTES
UNIVERSAL-INTERNATIONAL

DIRECTOR:	KURT NEUMANN	CAST	
PRODUCER:	LEONARD GOLDSTEIN		
ASSOCIATE PRODUCER:	ROSS HUNTER	TONY CURTIS	KASHMA BABA
SCREENPLAY:	GERALD DRAYSON ADAMS	PIPER LAURIE	AZURA/KIKI
ART DIRECTION:	BERNARD HERZBRUN AND	SUSAN CABOT	TALA
	EMRICH NICHOLSON	WILLIAM REYNOLDS	MUSTAFA
DIRECTOR OF PHOTOGRAPHY:	MAURY GERTSMAN	HUGH O'BRIAN	HUSSEIN
EDITOR:	VIRGIL VOGEL	VICTOR JORY	CALIPH
SOUND:	LESLIE I. CAREY AND GLENN E. ANDERSON	MORRIS ANKRUM	ALI BABA
PRODUCTION MANAGER:	EUGENE ANDERSON	PHILIP VAN ZANDT	KAREEB
MUSIC:	JOSEPH GERSHENSON	LEON BELASCO	BABU
COSTUMES:	ROSEMARY ODELL	PALMER LEE	FAROUK
		BARBARA KNUDSON	THEDA
		ALICE KELLEY	CALU

To capitalise on their sudden popularity as reflected in the fan mail, magazine coverage and box-office receipts from 'The Prince Who Was A Thief', Curtis and Laurie were speedily reunited on a second Arabian Knights adventure. Son of Ali Baba strictly adheres to a formula of a muscular young hero and plucky young heroine conquering all odds. The film's success proved that the reception to their first film was not a flash in the pan and that the acrobatic and fencing skills acquired by Curtis whilst being groomed for stardom had not been in vain.

Kashma Baba, son of Ali Baba, is a cadet at the Persian Imperial Military Academy where his deadliest rival is Hussein, son of the Caliph of Baghdad. The Caliph plots to acquire Ali Baba's great wealth and captures Princess Azura of Fez and her mother Princess Karma whilst they are en route to the palace of the Shah whom Azura was to have married. The Caliph threatens to torture Azura's mother unless Azura masquerades as a dancing girl Kiki and ingratiates her way into the household of Ali Baba. Azura accomplishes this and genuinely falls in love with Kashma. The Caliph then informs the Shah that she is being held against her will and that he will ride to her rescue.

The Caliph's men engage in combat with Ali Baba's forces and are victorious. Ali Baba's palace is burnt to the ground and he is taken prisoner and led to Baghdad. Kashma rallies the Sons of the Forty Thieves and, aided by his childhood sweetheart Tala, he storms the Caliph's palace rescuing his father and Princess Karma. During the battle Kashma kills Hussein and Tala dispatches the Caliph with a well-aimed arrow.

The Shah is informed of the Caliph's plot and Ali Baba is appointed in his place whilst Kashma and Azura are reunited in each others arms.

"The main roles are vivaciously played by Tony Curtis and Piper Laurie. (The) treatment makes confident entertainment with spirited action in the cloak and dagger style."

TODAY'S CINEMA

"Spacious, extravagant and disarmingly juvenile fun. Tony Curtis displays plenty of agility as Kashma."

KINEMATOGRAPH WEEKLY

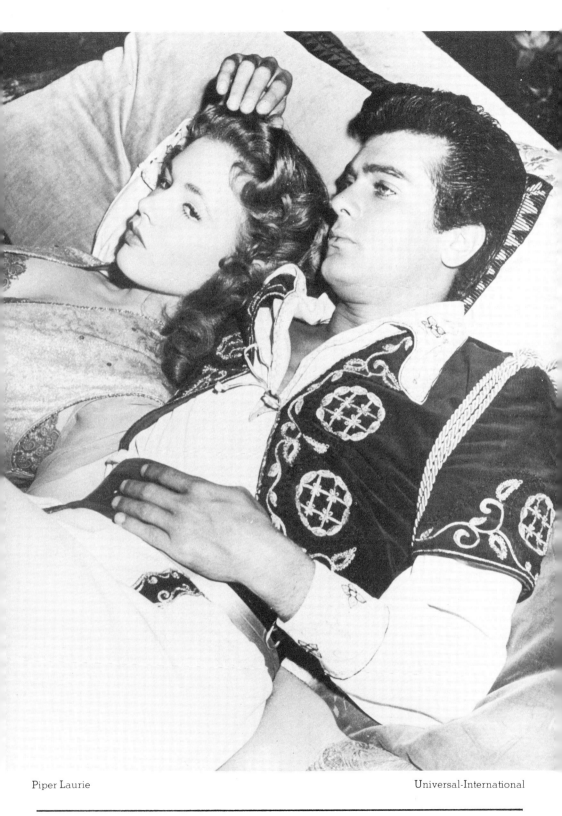

Piper Laurie

Universal-International

FLESH AND FURY

U.S.A. 1952 – RUNNING TIME: 82 MINUTES
UNIVERSAL-INTERNATIONAL

		CAST	
DIRECTOR	JOSEPH PEVNEY		
PRODUCER	LEONARD GOLDSTEIN		
SCREENPLAY:	BERNARD GORDON FROM A STORY	TONY CURTIS	PAUL CALLAN
	BY WILLIAM ALLAND	JAN STERLING	SONYA BARTOW
ART DIRECTION:	BERNARD HERZBRUN AND	MONA FREEMAN	ANN HOLLIS
	EMRICH NICHOLSON	WALLACE FORD	JACK RICHARDSON
DIRECTOR OF PHOTOGRAPHY:	IRVING GLASSBERG	CONNIE GILCHRIST	MRS RICHARDSON
EDITOR:	VIRGIL VOGEL	KATHERINE LOCKE	MRS HOLLIS
SOUND:	LESLIE I. CAREY AND ROBERT PRITCHARD	JOE GRAY	CLIFF
MUSIC:	HANS J. SALTER	RON HARGRAVE	AL LOGAN
COSTUMES:	BILL THOMAS	HARRY GUARDINO	LOU CALLAN
		HARRY SHANNON	MIKE CALLAN
		HARRY RAVEN	MURPH

The role of a deaf, mute boxer provided Curtis with a rare acting challenge from among his early screen assignments. In later years he would give good cause for recalling the filming under director Joseph Pevney. "There was this guy I was supposed to be boxing with, and he kept working me over unnecessarily, really making me angrier and angrier", he told the magazine Photoplay in 1979. "Then he really knocked me down. I felt a blind rage and an urge to smash him to pulp. I could have killed him right there. I stopped myself just in time."

Contemporary film reviewers often took Curtis to task for being little more than a pretty face. With 'Flesh and Fury' he began to receive grudging acknowledgement of his ability an an actor.

Paul Callan, a deaf mute, is a skilful boxer with the potential to be a champion. He is slavishly devoted to nightclub singer Sonya and uses his boxing earnings to shower her with gifts. Sonya enjoys the jewellery, the luxury apartment and the car that Paul provides but demands more and forces his manager, Jack Richardson, to agree to a contest with a 'dirty' fighter who may well seriously injure the young boxer.

During training in New Jersey Paul is interviewed by magazine writer Ann Hollis and accepts her invitation to go sailing. Ann shows a special sensitivity to Paul as her late father was also deaf. Encouraged by Ann's love and care Paul breaks away from Sonya and undergoes an operation which restores his hearing and enables him to learn to talk. He rushes to Ann's luxurious Long Island home to display his progress. She is overjoyed but Paul is overwhelmed by the noise and chatter of a party which is in progress. He feels that he is not suited to the same lifestyle as Ann and returns to Sonya.

Paul finally leaves Sonya when he discovers a telegram that she has hidden, informing him that any further fighting will probably result in the loss of his hearing again. Paul goes ahead with his championship fight and, although his hearing goes, he defeats the champion and wins the title. After the fight he is happily reunited with Ann. Then, as the couple stroll along the street Paul suddenly stops. Faintly, at first, but growing stronger he can hear the newsboys proclaiming his victory.

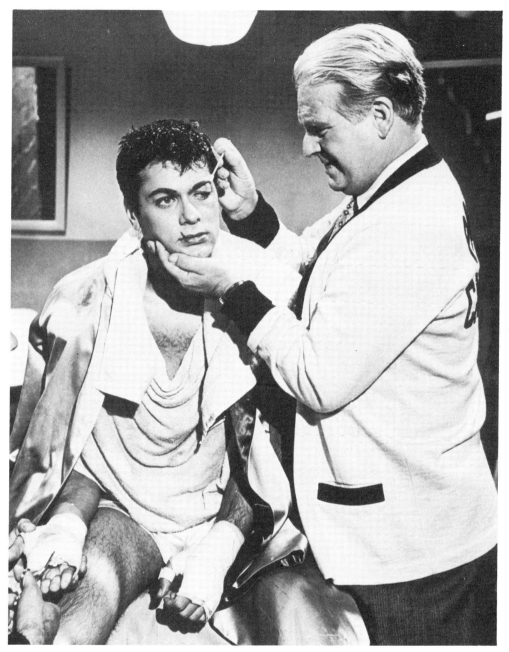

Wallace Ford (right)   Universal-International

"The picture, unlike most others touching on physical disability, makes its point without embarrassing its audience. Tony Curtis does a good job and distinguishes himself in the ring."
KINEMATOGRAPH WEEKLY

"There is Tony Curtis, who can box and who does a fine job of acting, both as a mute and as one who learns to talk and to hear. In fact, the picture gives a handsome Curtis for the women, and a skilful, fighting Curtis in some very convincing fight scenes for the men."
MOTION PICTURE HERALD

No Room For The Groom

U.S.A. 1952 – RUNNING TIME: 82 MINUTES
UNIVERSAL-INTERNATIONAL

DIRECTOR:	DOUGLAS SIRK	CAST	
PRODUCER:	TED RICHMOND		
SCREENPLAY:	JOSEPH HOFFMAN FROM A STORY	TONY CURTIS	ALVAH MORRELL
	'MY TRUE LOVE' BY DARWIN L. TEILHET	PIPER LAURIE	LEE KINGSHEAD
ART DIRECTION:	BERNARD HERZBRUN AND	DON DE FORE	HERMAN STROUPLE
	RICHARD H. RIEDEL	SPRING BYINGTON	MAMA KINGSHEAD
DIRECTOR OF PHOTOGRAPHY:	CLIFFORD STINE	JACK KELLY	WILL STUBBINS
EDITOR:	RUSSELL SCHOENGARTH	LEE AAKER	DONOVAN MURRAY
SOUND:	LESLIE I. CAREY AND CORSON JOWETT	LILLIAN BRONSON	AUNT ELSA
MUSIC:	FRANK SKINNER	STEPHEN CHASE	MR TAYLOR
COSTUMES:	BILL THOMAS	PAUL MCVEY	DR TROTTER
		FRANK SULLY	COUSIN LUKE

Curtis was always keen to expand his range as a performer and, perhaps because of his admiration for Cary Grant, light comedy was to prove one of his favourite genres. 'No Room for the Groom' is a nonsensical piece of froth — but nevertheless provides his first opportunity to develop a comic technique.

The director Douglas Sirk later became a cult figure of some standing for his vivid handling of Universal melodramas like 'Written on the Wind' (1956) and 'Imitation of Life' (1959). Piper Laurie would later recall him as being unsympathetic towards the inexperience of his young performers and a rather haughty, aloof figure.

Before returning to the Army Alvah Morrell elopes with his sweetheart Lee Kingshead to Las Vegas. However, as soon as they retire to the bridal suite Lee discovers a rash on Alvah's face and he is rushed to hospital with chickenpox. Alvah spends their honeymoon in hospital and is then shipped to Korea. Lee returns home to her mother in Suttersville keeping her marriage a secret.

One year later Alvah returns on leave. He finds that Lee, her mother and all her immediate relatives have moved into his large, rambling farmhouse and they're all working for local businessman Herman Strouple. Lee still hasn't told her mother about their marriage, being afraid of the effect on her health. In fact Mama Kingshead enjoys the most robust health but has a habit of fainting when things don't go her way. Alvah is forced to endure the intrusion of Lee's family and even shares a bed with a little monster called Donovan. In desperation he tells Mama Kingshead of their marriage; she collapses and threatens to have the marriage annulled.

Lee sides with her family and calls Alvah unpatriotic when he refuses to allow Herman to build a direct line across his property. She only comes to her senses when Herman engages a lawyer and a psychiatrist to have Alvah declared insane and allow Lee to handle his affairs. Lee now attempts to make amends and promises Alvah a night to remember together before he returns to the Army once again.

Piper Laurie   Universal-International

"Quietly amusing dialogue gives point to incidents and lively performances by well tried star team and versatile supporting cast give humanity and vitality to the lighthearted if improbable situations. Carefree general entertainment."

TODAY'S CINEMA

"The comedy is strained and tedious with only an occasionally bright spot meriting a chuckle. Curtis and Miss Laurie are generally satisfactory although former plays a big drunk sequence, what should have been his best comedy scene, very poorly."

VARIETY

HOUDINI

U.S.A. 1953 - RUNNING TIME: 106 MINUTES
PARAMOUNT

		CAST	
DIRECTOR:	GEORGE MARSHALL		
PRODUCER:	GEORGE PAL		
ASSOCIATE PRODUCER:	FRANK FREEMAN JNR.	TONY CURTIS	HOUDINI
SCREENPLAY:	PHILIP YORDAN FROM A BOOK BY	JANET LEIGH	BESS, HIS WIFE
	HAROLD KELLOCK	TORIN THATCHER	OTTO
ART DIRECTION:	HAL PEREIRA AND AL NOZAKI	ANGELA CLARKE	MRS WEISS
DIRECTOR OF PHOTOGRAPHY:	ERNEST LASZLO	SIG RUMAN	SCHULTZ
EDITOR:	GEORGE TOMASINI	MICHAEL PATE	DOOLEY
SOUND:	HARRY MILLS AND GENE GARVIN	PETER BALDWIN	FRED
MUSIC:	ROY WEBB	CONNIE GILCHRIST	MRS SCHULTZ
		DOUGLAS SPENCER	SIMMS

Houdini is more noteworthy as the first on-screen appearance of Curtis opposite his wife Janet Leigh than as an accurate biography of the famed escapologist. The production gave Curtis an opportunity to indulge a long held passion for magic and he spent a month prior to filming learning sleight of hand and illusions from a teacher. Such was his enthusiasm for the project that he claimed; "I would gladly do it for nothing."

In reality Harry Houdini died in hospital of peritonitis and the 1953 advertising campaign is symptomatic of the film's fanciful flamboyance. Posters proclaimed; "You won't escape! The thrilling, incredible real-life, death-defying exploits of the most fabulous dare-devil of all time!... every day he defied death... every night — he claimed his reward."

New York. Harry Houdini is a struggling young magician working as 'Bruto the Wild Man' at Schultz's Dime Museum when he first catches sight of Bess. The couple meet again, fall in love and marry. Initially Harry perseveres with his ambition to earn a living as a magician, but at Bess's heeding he takes a job with regular hours working in a safe and lock factory.

Harry's new job heightens his interest in escapology and, at a dinner given by the Society of Magicians, he frees himself from a straitjacket. The society offers him the chance to visit Europe and, eventually, Bess becomes resigned to Harry's obsession with magic. The couple sail for Britain and, in London, Harry creates a sensation by escaping from a seemingly impregnable jail. His fame spreads throughout Europe and, in Berlin, he attempts to contact Von Schweger; an old magician who had perfected a trick of escaping from a large sealed bottle. Before they can meet Von Schweger dies but his assistant Otto agrees to return to America with the Houdinis.

In America 'Houdini the Great' performs many death-defying stunts. On one occasion Harry is locked into a steel box and lowered into the frozen Detroit River. The stunt does not go according to plan but he hears his mother's voice calling him and is lead towards a safe opening in the ice. He later learns that his mother died at the same time that he had heard her voice. He retires from the stage for two years and genuinely tries to communicate with the dead. However, he only succeeds in exposing fake mediums and phoney seances. Returning to the stage Harry attempts to escape from a sealed tank of water. He is unable to perform the feat and, once rescued, dies in Bess's arms.

Janet Leigh   Paramount Productions

"Curtis and Miss Leigh make a winning team, playing the love scenes with moving tenderness and performing many of the magic tricks themselves."

HOLLYWOOD REPORTER

"In the title role, Tony Curtis is as unrevealing about Houdini the man as about Houdini the magician, hardly hinting at his dynamic personality, strength, ingenuity and resourcefulness."

TIME

With firmer direction, and with make-up that indicated ageing through more than powdered temples, Tony Curtis and Janet Leigh might well have been convincing."

MONTHLY FILM BULLETIN

THE ALL-AMERICAN

UK TITLE: THE WINNING WAY

U.S.A. 1953 – RUNNING TIME: 83 MINUTES
UNIVERSAL-INTERNATIONAL

DIRECTOR:	JESSE HIBBS	**CAST**	
PRODUCER:	AARON ROSENBERG		
ASSOCIATE PRODUCER:	WILLIAM D. POWELL	**TONY CURTIS**	NICK BONELLI
SCREENPLAY:	D.D. BEAUCHAMP FROM A STORY BY	**LORI NELSON**	SHARON WALLACE
	LEONARD FREEMAN	**RICHARD LONG**	HOWARD CARTER
ART DIRECTION:	BERNARD HERZBRUN AND	**MAMIE VAN DOREN**	SUSIE WARD
	ERIC ORBOM	**GREGG PALMER**	HUNT CAMERON
DIRECTORY OF PHOTOGRAPHY:	MAURY GERTSMAN	**PAUL CAVANAGH**	PROFESSOR BANNING
EDITOR:	EDWARD CURTISS	**HERMAN HICKMAN**	JUMBO CAMPBELL
SOUND:	LESLIE I. CAREY AND CORSON JOWETT	**MORGAN JONES**	CASEY
PRODUCTION MANAGER:	LEW LEARY	**STUART WHITMAN**	ZIP PARKER
MUSIC:	JOSEPH GERSHENSON	**JIMMY HUNT**	WHIZZER
COSTUMES:	ROSEMARY ODELL		

As a mark of the pace at which Curtis was working at Universal 'The All-American' went into production in April 1953, was reviewed by the critics in July, and ready for release to coincide with the start of the football season that autumn. Producer Aaron Rosenberg had been an All-American in 1933 and director Jesse Hibbs accomplished the same feat in 1927. To add further authenticity to the proceedings several former and current All-Americas were included within the cast line-up.

The film's release in Britain was delayed until 1955 when it appeared with a running time of 70 minutes; many scenes of American football having been cut by a distributor wary of British antipathy to the sport.

After his spectacular football playing in a Mid State vs Carolina game Nick Bonelli is awarded the much-coveted title of All-American. However, on the day of the game his parents are killed in a bus accident and Nick determines to reject his football skills and study architecture as his father had always wanted.

He wins a scholarship to Sheridan University with the aid of family friend David Carter but his surly personality does not endear him to his fellow students — especially when he will not join the football team. At the Pewter Mug, an 'off limits' pub, Nick comes to blows with Howard Carter, David's son. When the matter is brought to the attention of the Dean Nick denies the incident and Howard is placed on probation. However, the Dean's secretary Sharon Wallace takes an interest in Nick and persuades him to return to football. Nick proves himself a valuable team member and is invited to join the Campus Club at the same time as Howard, who has been acting in a very unsportsmanlike manner, is asked to leave.

On the day of the big game against Mid State Nick learns that David Carter is coming to see his son play unaware of Howard's fall from grace. Nick finds Howards at the Pewter Mug but is knocked unconscious by a waitress and, when discovered by the police, is expelled from University. Before leaving he persuades the coach to let Howard play.

Sharon learns the truth of why Nick had gone to the Pewter Mug and he is reinstated. Playing in harmony for once Nick and Howard lead their team to victory and, after the game, Nick finds Sharon waiting for him.

Lori Nelson   Universal-International

"Here is an exciting campus yarn built around the college sport that rates with any football film yet made... Curtis is thoroughly believable as a football star."

HOLLYWOOD REPORTER

"This rah-rah football feature with Tony Curtis as a star quarterback is an entertaining offering. While no great classic... it is plenty of fun."

VARIETY

FORBIDDEN

U.S.A. 1953 - RUNNING TIME: 85 MINUTES
UNIVERSAL-INTERNATIONAL

		CAST	
DIRECTOR:	RUDOLPH MATÉ		
PRODUCER:	TED RICHMOND		
SCREENPLAY:	WILLIAM SACKHEIM AND GIL DOUD	TONY CURTIS	EDDIE DARROW
ART DIRECTION:	BERNARD HERZBRUN AND	JOANNE DRU	CHRISTINE LAWRENCE
	RICHARD H. RIEDEL	LYLE BETTGER	JUSTIN KEIT
DIRECTOR OF PHOTOGRAPHY:	WILLIAM DANIELS	MARVIN MILLER	CLIFF CHALMER
EDITOR:	EDWARD CURTISS	VICTOR SEN YUNG	ALLAN
SOUND:	LESLIE I. CAREY AND JOE LAPIS	ALAN DEXTER	BARNEY
MUSIC:	FRANK SKINNER	DAVID SHARPE	LEON
COSTUMES:	BILL THOMAS	PETER MAMAKOS	SAM
		HOWARD CHUMAN	HON-FAI
		WEAVER LEVY	TANG
		HAROLD FONG	WONG
		MAI TAI SING	SOO LEE

Polish-born director Rudolph Maté worked with Curtis on several occasions and had been behind the helm of 'The Prince Who Was a Thief'. 'Forbidden' is a standard thriller and star vehicle for Curtis.

The leading lady, former model Joanne Dru, had enjoyed a fairly promising early film career with appearances in 'Red River' (1948), 'All the King's Men' (1949) and two films by John Ford. However, by the time of 'Forbidden' her best films were all behind her.

Eddie Darrow is hired by gangster Barney Pendleton to travel to Macao and retrieve some potentially incriminating documents from Christine Lawrence, Darrow's former girlfriend. In Macao Eddie is employed by Justin Keit at his club. Eddie is amazed to discover that Christine is Keit's fiancee. Later, when the two find time to talk, Christine explains that she has clung to Keit for protection and Eddie makes plans for both of them to double cross Pendleton and start a new life in Australia.

Meanwhile, Pendleton has dispatched Cliff Chalmer to Macao to ensure that a double-cross does not occur. Eddie attempts to deceive Chalmer by claiming that the Australian trip is merely an excuse to get Christine on a boat to America. Christine overhears this explanation, and, believing it to be true, is heartbroken and agrees to marry Keit. Chalmer believes that the marriage will hinder Christine's return to America and decides to kill Keit. However, in a shoot out, it is Keit who kills him.

Eddie and Christine attempt to escape on board the freighter SS Malabar hotly pursued by Keit's henchmen. A wild gunshot ignites the high combustion wheat dust in the ship's hold and the vessel is destroyed but not before Eddie and Christine reach safety. Searching the wreckage officials discover Christine's purse and she is listed among the dead. Eddie and Christine board another liner heading for America and a fresh start together.

"Tony Curtis gets himself involved in considerable running around in Macao as this dramatic number hits its stride. Adapting himself capably enough to the dramatic requirements of an unusual role Curtis rather carries the burden of the script."

FILM DAILY

"This violent and unpleasant story, enacted against a background of glossy luxury clubs and apartments, has almost nothing to commend it. Directed with a cold and impersonal touch by Rudolph Maté, it contains a very inept performance by Tony Curtis and a philosophical Chinese piano player who talks like one of Charlie Chan's sons."

MONTHLY FILM BULLETIN

Joanne Dru

Universal-International

BEACHHEAD

U.S.A. 1954 - RUNNING TIME: 89 MINUTES
AUBREY SCHENCK PRODUCTION FOR UNITED ARTISTS

		CAST	
DIRECTOR:	STUART HEISLER		
PRODUCER:	HOWARD KOCH		
SCREENPLAY:	RICHARD ALAN SIMMONS FROM	TONY CURTIS	BURKE
	THE NOVEL 'I'VE GOT MINE' BY	FRANK LOVEJOY	SGT. FLETCHER
	RICHARD G. HUBLER	MARY MURPHY	NINA
DIRECTOR OF PHOTOGRAPHY:	GORDON AVIL	EDUARD FRANZ	BOUCHARD
EDITOR:	JOHN F. SCHREYER	SKIP HOMEIER	REYNOLDS
MUSIC:	EMIL NEWMAN AND ARTHUR LANGE	JOHN DOUCETTE	MAJOR SCOTT
COSTUMES:	WESLEY V. JEFFRIES	ALAN WELLS	BIGGERMAN

A distinctly above average war film 'Beachhead' was given added distinction by the colour photography by Gordon Avil and by the fact that it was shot entirely on location in Kauai among the Hawaiian islands. Curtis again surprised many with his forceful performance as a resentful young marine.

World War II. Four marines are sent on a hazardous mission to ascertain the veracity of radio reports from French planter Bouchard regarding a Japanese minefield. Proceeding through the island jungle two of the party are killed leaving Burke and the veteran sergeant Fletcher. The two soldiers come across a jungle clearing and discover the plantation. Fletcher prepares to kill the one human being they encounter until he realises that it is Nina Bouchard. Nina leads the marines to her father's hiding place and Bouchard verifies his radio messages.

The group heads for a radio shack near the coast to make contact with the main body of the marine forces. However, they are attacked before a message can be sent and are forced to undertake an exhausting journey towards a coastal rendezvous. On the journey Nina injures her ankle and virtually slows their progress to a halt. Fletcher decides that the best policy is for Burke to carry on alone and return with help. At this moment Bouchard is killed by a sniper's bullet. Fletcher sends Burke on ahead with Nina and remains behind to deal with the sniper. Fletcher ruthlessly spurs them on to reach the beach. Their hopes of rescue are dashed when they sight a Japanese gun barge. Burke however, wades into the water and destroys the barge with a hand grenade. Fletcher pulls him out of the ensuing conflagration. A large body of soldiers appears on the horizon and the trio fear the worst — but the soldiers turn out to be United States marines. Nina is transferred to a hospital ship whilst Burke and Fletcher await their next assignment together have developed a mutual appreciation.

"Curtis turns in his best job yet, giving his role an intelligent mixture of toughness and good humour."

VARIETY

"This is a picture which deals with neurosis, brutality, bravery, lust, unselfishness and despite such a mixture it achieves a sense of truth. One hesitates to flog a word but this picture has integrity. Tony Curtis and Frank Lovejoy are first class as the case-hardened sergeant and the ardent, bitter young marine."

EVENING STANDARD

"You catch undertones not only of the errie terror of the jungle with Japs lurking everywhere but of the smouldering resentment which develops among the marines... The film belongs to the two marines played by Tony Curtis and Frank Lovejoy."

NEWS OF THE WORLD

Mary Murphy and Frank Lovejoy   Aubrey Schenck Productions

JOHNNY DARK

U.S.A. 1954 – RUNNING TIME: 85 MINUTES
UNIVERSAL-INTERNATIONAL

		CAST	
DIRECTOR:	GEORGE SHERMAN		
PRODUCER:	WILLIAM ALLAND		
SCREENPLAY:	FRANKLIN COEN	TONY CURTIS	JOHNNY DARK
ART DIRECTION:	BERNARD HERZBRUN AND	PIPER LAURIE	LIZ FIELDING
	ROBERT BOYLE	DON TAYLOR	DUKE BENSON
DIRECTOR OF PHOTOGRAPHY:	CARL GUTHRIE	PAUL KELLY	JIM 'SCOTTY' SCOTT
EDITOR:	EDWARD CURTISS	ILKA CHASE	ABBIE BINNS
SOUND:	LESLIE I. CAREY AND	SIDNEY BLACKMER	JAMES FIELDING
	GLENN E. ANDERSON	RUTH HAMPTON	MISS BORDER-TO-BORDER
PRODUCTION MANAGER:	SERGEI PETSCHNIKOFF	RUSSELL JOHNSON	EMORY
MUSIC:	JOSEPH GERSHENSON	JOE SAWYER	SVENSON
COSTUMES:	JAY MORLEY JNR.	ROBERT NICHOLS	SMITTY

A well-tailored vehicle for the popular team of Curtis and Piper Laurie, 'Johnny Dark' was the duo's final appearance together. Like Curtis Laurie longed to prove her value as a serious actress and was soon to forsake Hollywood for the rigours of stage work and live television in New York. Over the years she has found many settings for her considerable talent and has twice been nominated for the Academy Award as Best Actress in 'The Hustler' (1961) and Best Supporting Actress in 'Carrie' (1976).

'Johnny Dark' was reworked a decade later into the film 'The Lively Set' starring James Darren, Pamela Tiffin and Doug McClure.

At Fielding Motors tension grows between founder President James Fielding and the company stockholders. Chief engineer Jim Scott shows Fielding plans for a new type of sports car designed by one of the employees — Johnny Dark. Fielding agrees to build the car as a sop to the stockholders although he has no intention of putting it into production.

Johnny eagerly applies himself to bringing his designs to life, unaware that the car is a one-off. He is aided by Scott, top test driver Duke Benson and Fielding's daughter Liz. When their work is finished Johnny's hopes of future developments are dashed; the car will not receive official company status and cannot be entered in a forthcoming race. Disillusioned that all his work has been in vain he leaves the company. Scott has faith in Johnny's plans and steals the car, thus enabling Duke to enter the race. The car just fails to win, largely because of Duke's reckless driving which leads to a crash. Johnny and Duke quarrel and part company.

Johnny and his crew repair the car and enter it in a three-day race from Canada to Mexico. During the race the car more than proves its worth until a minor accident threatens to deny Johnny victory. Fielding is won over to the idea that the car will be good for the company and sends a team of specialist mechanics who help Johnny to victory ahead of Duke, now the leader of a rival team. Johnny and Duke renew their friendship, Johnny and Liz plan to marry and Fielding announces that the car will go into production immediately.

"Aided by the pleasant personalities of its youthful performers this formula picture tells its story with a good deal of unpretentious charm." **MONTHLY FILM BULLETIN**

Piper Laurie   Universal-International

"Johnny Dark will lighten a great many hearts. This industry can't have too many pictures to lure back young audiences, in presenting this exciting comedy of youth and speed and the open road William Alland has turned out one of his best.

He (Sherman) uses the pertness of Miss Laurie's profile and the good-natured persistance of Mr Curtis's personality in a way that will delight the public that reads, avidly, of all their more important doings in the fan magazines."

                                                HOLLYWOOD REPORTER

THE BLACK SHIELD OF FALWORTH

U.S.A. 1954 – RUNNING TIME: 99 MINUTES
UNIVERSAL-INTERNATIONAL

		CAST	
DIRECTOR:	RUDOLPH MATÉ		
PRODUCERS:	ROBERT ARTHUR AND		
	MELVILLE TUCKER	TONY CURTIS	MYLES FALWORTH
SCREENPLAY:	OSCAR BRODNEY FROM	JANET LEIGH	LADY ANN
	THE NOVEL 'MEN OF IRON' BY	DAVID FARRAR	EARL OF ALBAN
	HOWARD PYLE	BARBARA RUSH	MEG FALWORTH
ART DIRECTION:	ALEXANDER GOLITZEN AND	CRAIG HILL	FRANCIS GASCOYNE
	RICHARD H. RIEDEL	HERBERT MARSHALL	EARL OF MACKWORTH
DIRECTOR OF PHOTOGRAPHY:	IRVING GLASSBERG	RHYS WILLIAMS	DICCON BOWMAN
EDITOR:	TED J. KENT	DANIEL O'HERLIHY	PRINCE HAL
SOUND:	LESLIE I. CAREY AND JOE LAPIS	TORIN THATCHER	SIR JAMES
MUSIC:	JOSEPH GERSHENSON	IAN KEITH	KING HENRY IV
COSTUMES:	ROSEMARY ODELL		

'The Black Shield of Falworth' holds the distinction of being Universal's first production in the new process of Cinemascope. When film attendances began to drop in the 1950s the major studios turned to lavish epics, short-lived gimmicks like 3-D, and attempts to alter the size of the screen in order to hold the viewers' attention. Cinemascope gave a larger, wider picture but meant that the camera remained somewhat static.

England. The King is ailing and the real power in the land lies with the wicked Earl of Alban. The Earl of Macworth is no friend of Alban's and plots with the good Prince Hal to undermine Alban's influence. Orphans Myles and Meg Falworth are entered into service at Macworth Castle, Meg as a lady-in-waiting to the fair Lady Ann and Myles to train as a squire and, later, as a knight. Myles is aware of a closely-guarded secret regarding their parentage but has only a mysterious coat of arms as a clue to his past.

Myles continues his training under the exacting Sir James visiting Lady Ann every day. She however, is pledged to marry Alban's brother. Eventually the Earl of Macworth tells Myles that he is of noble birth. His father was the Earl of Falworth who was unjustly branded a traitor and slain by the Earl of Alban who now owns the estate that rightfully belongs to Myles and Meg.

King Henry and his entourage visit Macworth Castle where Myles is knighted to enable him to joust for his country. When Myles carries the outlawed colours of Falworth into battle Alban demands his arrest. Instead Myles is allowed to defend the family name in trial by combat. He is victorious, killing Alban, while his friend Francis Gascoyne and the other squires triumph over Alban's supporters. The King restores Myles' title and estate and blesses his marriage to Lady Ann.

"What is important is that it has love, romance, movement and the staunch heroics that please mass audiences. Tony Curtis leads nimble vigor to his role of a young peasant."
MOTION PICTURE HERALD

"He is possibly one of the few belted knights in history to say mayhap with a Brooklyn accent."
TIME

"As the bold English knight, Tony Curtis reveals great athletic prowess and much determination, but, alas, his voice betrays him… Altogether, a straight-forward piece of hokum, with no pretentions, and spoken in a variety of accents that only Hollywood could muster."
MONTHLY FILM BULLETIN

Janet Leigh   Universal-International

TONY CURTIS **51**

SO THIS IS PARIS

U.S.A. 1954 – RUNNING TIME: 96 MINUTES
UNIVERSAL-INTERNATIONAL

		CAST	
DIRECTOR:	RICHARD QUINE		
PRODUCER:	ALBERT J. COHEN		
SCREENPLAY:	CHARLES HOFFMAN FROM A	TONY CURTIS	JOE MAXWELL
	STORY BY RAY BUFFUM	GLORIA DE HAVEN	COLETTE D'AVRIL/
ART DIRECTION:	ALEXANDER GOLITZEN		JANIE MITCHELL
	AND EUGENE LORIE	GENE NELSON	AL HOWARD
DIRECTOR OF PHOTOGRAPHY:	MAURY GERTSMAN	CORINNE CALVET	SUZANNE SOREL
EDITOR	VIRGIL VOGEL	PAUL GILBERT	DAVEY JONES
SOUND:	LESLIE I. CAREY AND	MARA CORDAY	YVONNE
	ROBERT PRITCHARD	ALLISON HAYES	CARMEN
MUSIC:	JOSEPH GERSHENSON	CHRISTIANE MARTEL	CHRISTIANE
COSTUMES:	ROSEMARY ODELL	MYRNE HANSEN	INGRID
CHOREOGRAPHY:	GENE NELSON AND LEE SCOTT	ROGER ETIENNE	PIERRE DESHONS

With the exceptions of the films of Deanna Durbin and Donald O'Connor Universal was never a studio renowned for its musical output. In the 1930s RKO had Astaire and Rogers, Warner Brothers had Dick Powell and Ruby Keeler whilst MGM was dominant throughout the entire history of the 'dream factory' years, employing talents like Judy Garland and Gene Kelly. So This is Paris is a bargain-basement mixture of 'On the Town' and 'An American in Paris'. The film has verve and energy and Curtis emerges as a creditable song and dance man in his only leading role in a musical. Whilst other studios lavished money and time on their productions 'So This is Paris' was completed, economically and expertly, in just 22 days.

Paris. Joe Maxwell, Al Howard and Davey Jones, three American sailors, are on leave and determined to make every minute count. At a bistro on the Left Bank Joe meets Janie Mitchell, also known as Colette d'Avril, the cafe's star attraction. Davey becomes involved with the cashier Yvonne. Later on Al comes to the rescue of heiress Suzanne Monet, when a thief tries to steal her purse, and is invited to her home.

Janie invites the three sailors to lunch where they are introduced to her French grandmother and the six war orphans who live with them. The trio journey on to Suzanne's mansion. Joe is smitten with the heiress who subsequently announces their engagement to the press. Janie vows never to see Joe again.

Janie receives news that the wealthy American benefactor who has provided for the orphans over the years is dead and there will be no further remittances until his estate is settled. By a happy coincidence the sailors used to have a nightclub act and decide to put on a fund-raising show for the orphans at Suzanne's mansion during her absence. When Suzanne and her father unexpectedly return they angrily demand an explanation of the events. They refuse to believe the story of the orphans until Al persuades Janie to bring the children to the show. Suzanne's father relents and allows the show to proceed. Everything goes well and a large sum of money is accumulated. After the excitement is over Janie is back with Joe, Davey has Yvonne with him and Al and Suzanne rediscover each other.

Gloria De Haven and Gene Nelson   Universal-International

"The material of this musical is conventional, but it emerges as an entertainment well above average in gusto and skill. The whole film has a confident, invigorating pace and bite; numbers are staged with precision and sometimes - with brilliance. Tony Curtis, Gene Nelson and Paul Gilbert clown, prowl, sing and dance with high spirits and good humour."

MONTHLY FILM BULLETIN

SIX BRIDGES TO CROSS

U.S.A. 1954 – RUNNING TIME: 96 MINUTES
UNIVERSAL-INTERNATIONAL

DIRECTOR:	JOSEPH PEVNEY	
PRODUCER:	AARON ROSENBERG	
SCREENPLAY:	SIDNEY BOEHM FROM THE NOVEL	
	'THEY STOLE $2,5000,000 — AND	
	GOT AWAY WITH IT' BY JOSEPH DINEEN	
ART DIRECTION:	ALEXANDER GOLITZEN	
	AND ROBERT CLATWORTHY	
DIRECTOR OF PHOTOGRAPHY:	WILLIAM DANIELS	
EDITOR:	RUSSELL SCHOENGARTH	
SOUND:	LESLIE I. CAREY AND JOE LAPIS	
PRODUCTION MANAGER:	DICK MCWHORTER	
MUSIC:	JOSEPH GERSHENSON	
COSTUMES:	JAY MORLEY JNR.	

CAST

TONY CURTIS	JERRY FLOREA
JULIE ADAMS	ELLEN GALLAGHER
GEORGE NADER	EDWARD GALLAGHER
JAY C. FLIPPEN	VINCENT CONCANNON
SAL MINEO	JERRY, AS A BOY
JAN MERLIN	ANDY NORRIS
WILLIAM MURPHY	RED FLANAGAN
KENNY ROBERTS	RED, AS A BOY
RICHARD CASTLE	SKIDS RADZIEVICH

Over the years Curtis has been called upon to essay more than his fair share of petty hoodlums and vicious mobsters. Referring to his own poverty-stricken background and the road to crime followed by some of his contemporaries Curtis would comment; "There but for the grace of God go I."

'Six Bridges to Cross' was based on the famous Brinks robbery of 1950 once judged 'the perfect crime'. The production company ventured to Boston for location work and the film marked the acting debut of the young Sal Mineo who plays Curtis as a boy. The title song has music by Henry Mancini and is performed by Sammy Davis Jnr.

Boston, 1933. Young policeman Ed Gallagher attempts to stop a robbery and is forced to shoot Jerry Florea. Gallagher is labelled 'gun happy' by the press but receives praise from his superior. He visits Jerry in hospital and they form a friendship. Jerry is given twelve months probation and repays Gallagher by informing on a rival gang.

Jerry continues his life of crime. When a young girl leaves him for another gang member she accuses him of statutory rape although Andy Norris is really the guilty party. Jerry will not name his friend and is sent to prison.

During the war Gallagher joins the forces while Jerry announces his marriage to a lovely widow Virginia and claims that his criminal life-style is over. Later, when a sensational robbery takes place at an Armed Car Service plant near Jerry's office Florea becomes a prime suspect, as does Gallagher because of his long association with the former gangster.

Gallagher is convinced that Jerry can identify those responsible for the robbery. He uses the fact that Jerry has neglected to mention his conviction for rape on official documents to instigate deportation proceedings. Gallagher locates Norris and forces a confession from him promising Jerry that he will hand over the confession in return for the information. However, legally Gallagher cannot withhold the confession and Jerry is released.

Jerry returns home but Virginia has left with the step-children, sickened by his attitude. Jerry decides to lead Gallagher to the stolen money and turn himself in. He intends to warn the other members of the gang first but there is an argument and he is shot. Gallagher arrives to arrest the gang and recover the money. Jerry dies in the detective's arms.

Universal-International

"Curtis gives the character a good reading, rating a modicum of sympathy even though viewers know he is unregenerated and must die at the finale."

VARIETY

"The film belongs to Florea. And as that brash bandit is played by crew-cut Tony Curtis with his continual twisted smile I need say no more."

NEWS OF THE WORLD

THE PURPLE MASK

U.S.A. 1955 - RUNNING TIME: 82 MINUTES
UNIVERSAL-INTERNATIONAL

DIRECTOR:	BRUCE HUMBERSTONE	**CAST**
PRODUCER:	HOWARD CHRISTIE	
SCREENPLAY:	OSCAR BRODNEY BASED ON THE	
	PLAY BY PAUL ARMONT AND JEAN MANOUSSI	
ART DIRECTION:	ALEXANDER GOLITZEN AND	
	ERIC ORBOM	
DIRECTOR OF PHOTOGRAPHY:	IRVING GLASSBERG	
EDITOR:	TED J. KENT	
SOUND:	LESLIE I. CAREY AND	
	GLENN E. ANDERSON	
MUSIC:	JOSEPH GERSHENSON	
COSTUMES:	BILL THOMAS	

TONY CURTIS	RENÉ
COLLEEN MILLER	LAURETTE
GENE BARRY	CAPTAIN LAWRENCE
DAN O'HERLIHY	BRISQUET
ANGELA LANSBURY	MME VALENTINE
GEORGE DOLENZ	MARCEL CARDONAL
JOHN HOYT	FOUCHE
MYRNA HANSEN	CONSTANCE
PAUL CAVANAGH	DUC DE LATOUR
ALLISON HAYES	IRENE
JANE HOWARD	YVONNE

Curtis's last overt swashbuckler until 'The Count of Monte Cristo' almost twenty years later, 'The Purple Mask' is an entertaining piece of nonsense which wastes some good performers like Angela Lansbury who claimed; "I needed the money so badly that I played a seamstress in a Tony Curtis film."

The Universal publicity department noted that Curtis and Janet Leigh moved into a new house during the filming of 'The Purple Mask' and, such was their popularity, that they were showered with gifts from fans. One gift reported was a frozen side of beef from a farmer in Dodge City who wrote; "Kinda thought you might be out of ready money with all the expenses of a new house. This will keep you eating."

Paris, 1802. France is ruled by the dictatorship of Napoleon and it is a period of persecution for supporters of the monarchy. A defender of the Royalists has arisen in the guise of the mysterious, dashing Purple Mask, otherwise known as Count René de Trevieres an effete fop who is a seemingly insignificant figure in the Royalist struggle. His success in saving Royalists from the guillotine angers Napoleon who appoints Brisquet to capture the Purple Mask. He proves incompetent and falls victim to the elusive hero.

Laurette de Latour has been working for a Royalist underground movement with her father Duc de Latour. When the group is captured she is taken prisoner and condemned to death — but not for long as she happens to be the woman that the Purple Mask loves. Unfortunately René is also captured but Laurette is content to face death with him when she learns his true identity.

Fellow Royalists come to the rescue of the condemned group and the Purple Mask is allowed to duel with Brisquet for the freedom of his friends. René wins the duel and Napoleon allows the group to set sail for freedom and happiness across the English Channel in Britain.

"Tony Curtis plays the leading role with a playful subtlety that should please his fans and he is graceful and convincing in the duelling scenes."

HOLLYWOOD REPORTER

"This costumed swashbuckler is right out of the Scarlet Pimpernel with Tony Curtis doing swordplay. Curtis is an acceptable hero, making the best of the dual characterization, while Miss Miller is a pretty heroine.

VARIETY

Universal-International

"Tony Curtis's evident decision to refuse to take seriously this ponderous piece of ''period'' writing was perhaps a wise one. The result is an engaging single turn which leaves the rest of the cast to their fate."

MONTHLY FILM BULLETIN

THE SQUARE JUNGLE

U.S.A. 1955 – RUNNING TIME: 86 MINUTES
UNIVERSAL-INTERNATIONAL

DIRECTOR:	JERRY HOPPER	CAST	
PRODUCER:	ALBERT ZUGSMITH		
SCREENPLAY:	GEORGE ZUCKERMAN	TONY CURTIS	EDDIE QUAID
ART DIRECTION:	ALEXANDER GOLITZEN AND		(PACKY GLENNON)
	AL SWEENEY	PAT CROWLEY	JULIE WALSH
DIRECTOR OF PHOTOGRAPHY:	GEORGE ROBINSON	ERNEST BORGNINE	BERNIE BROWN
EDITOR:	PAUL WEATHERWAX	PAUL KELLY	JIM MCBRIDE
SOUND:	LESLIE I. CAREY AND	JIM BACKUS	PAT QUAID
	JOHN KEAN	LEIGH SNOWDEN	LORRAINE EVANS
PRODUCTION MANAGER:	SERGEI PETSCHINKOFF	JOHN DAY	AL GORSKI
MUSIC:	HEINZ ROEMHELD	JOE VITALE	TONY ADAMSON
COSTUMES:	ROSEMARY ODELL	JOHN MARLEY	TOMMY DILLON
		DAVID JANSSEN	JACK LINDSEY

When Curtis's co-star Ernest Borgnine received surprise acclaim, and later an Oscar, for his gentle Bronx butcher in 'Marty' (1955) there was a hasty addition to the advertising posters of 'The Square Jungle', a competent second feature, accentuating the 'wonderful star of Marty'. In many of his films Curtis is complemented by a strong supporting cast as he is here in 'The Square Jungle'. Aside from Borgnine the film provides a strong role for Jim Backus as the weak-willed father in the same year as a similar role in the memorable 'Rebel Without a Cause'. The film has an authentic boxing flavour and Joe Louis appears as himself.

San Francisco. Young Eddie Quaid works as a grocery clerk and lives with his widowed father Pat, a lorry driver whose bouts of alcoholism have left him unable to find work. One evening when Eddie is on a date with his girl Julie his father becomes involved in a brawl and is arrested. Julie's father, wealthy businessman Mike Walsh, learns of the incident and tells Eddie that he must never see Julie again.

Eddie lacks the money to pay his father's bail and enters a boxing contest to raise the funds. Unknown to Eddie detective Jim McBride arranges for his father to see the fight, hoping to shame him into renouncing his alcoholism. Eddie wins the fight and shows considerable potential as a boxer. McBride offers Eddie the chance to make boxing his career and introduces him to trainer Bernie Brown. Eddie trains hard, hoping to forget Julie. He quickly rises to become middleweight champion of the world. Julie's father is now dead and she appears at a party given to celebrate Eddie's success. However, Eddie merely insults her.

Eddie's success continues and he becomes blinded by self-importance until a rematch with the former champion Al Gorski. Eddie knocks out his opponent who is rushed to hospital critically ill. Gorski lives but is ordered to stop boxing. Eddie retires from the ring and refuses to see anyone. However, with the help of Julie and Bernie Brown he is persuaded to return to the public eye and meets Gorski at a boxing stadium. Both are spectators and use the meeting to patch up their differences. Eddie finds he can face the world again with Julie by his side.

Pat Crowley   Universal-International

"Tony Curtis piles up a telling score of points for himself as a performer and a box-office power in this trim tale of a boxer who learns more than the manly art of self defense from a trainer quite as tellingly played by Ernest Borgnine."

MOTION PICTURE HERALD

"Curtis responds well to the directorial demands of Jerry Hopper as a young man who turns to the ring to raise bail money for his drunken father and goes on to become middleweight champion."

VARIETY

THE RAWHIDE YEARS

U.S.A. 1955 – RUNNING TIME: 85 MINUTES
UNIVERSAL-INTERNATIONAL

DIRECTOR:	RUDOLPH MATÉ	CAST
PRODUCER:	STANLEY RUBIN	
SCREENPLAY:	EARL FELTON FROM A NOVEL	TONY CURTIS — BEN MATTHEWS
	BY NORMAN A. FOX	COLLEEN MILLER — ZOE
ART DIRECTION:	ALEXANDER GOLITZEN AND	ARTHUR KENNEDY — RICK HARPER
	RICHARD H. RIEDEL	WILLIAM DEMAREST — BRAND COMFORT
DIRECTOR OF PHOTOGRAPHY:	IRVING GLASSBERG	WILLIAM GARGAN — MARSHAL SOMMERS
EDITOR:	RUSSELL SCHOENGARTH	PETER VAN EYCK — ANTOINE BOUCHER
SOUND:	LESLIE I. CAREY AND	MINOR WATSON — MATT COMFORT
	ROBERT PRITCHARD	DONALD RANDOLPH — CARRICO
MUSIC:	FRANK SKINNER AND	CHUBBY JOHNSON — GIF LESSING
	HANS J. SALTER	JAMES ANDERSON — DEPUTY WADE
COSTUMES:	BILL THOMAS	

Universal certainly extracted value for money from Curtis and, coincidentally, allowed him to learn his craft in every conceivable genre.'The Rawhide Years' represents his one starring role in a western. According to the Universal publicity department Colleen Miller, who had previously co-starred with Curtis in 'The Purple Mask', had been a member of the San Francisco Tony Curtis Fan Club before entering the profession herself. She sings several songs in the film including 'Gypsy with the Fire in his Shoes' by Peggy Lee and 'Laurindo Almeida'.

The 1870s. Ben Matthews earns his living aboard the Mississippi steamboats as an accomplice to professional gambler Carrico. Ben observes the other players' cards and passes on the information to Carrico by a system of prearranged signals. However, he is upset by the losses of one old man and double-crosses Carrico thus ending the partnership. He is befriended by a fellow passenger, Matt Comfort. That evening Comfort is murdered and gunmen steal a wooden statue from his cabin. Ben discovers the body and is attacked by the robbers one of whom slashes his face with a metal-lined gun belt. Carrico is accused of the murder and is lynched by an angry mob. Ben is sought as an accomplice but manages to escape with the aid of his girlfriend, saloon entertainer Zoe. He vows to return and clear his name.

Three years later Ben returns partnered by easy-going wanderer Rick Harper. He suspects that Matt was murdered by his brother Brand Comfort who was conspiring with Antoine, Zoe's boss. He sets about finding the evidence to prove his suspicions. As he is about to accuse Brand and Antoine the latter attempts to ferment crowd hysteria and almost succeeds in lynching Rick. However, Ben intervenes and during a shoot-out Antoine is fatally wounded and confesses his crimes before expiring.

Ben's name is now cleared and he is ready to settle down to a new life with Zoe. Rick inherits his horse and rides off to continue his wandering life.

"Tony Curtis, as the young gambler-turned-honest, is very good, showing a flair for comedy that has seldom been exploited and the ability to carry his own in an outdoor, rough-and-tumble western. This young actor can apparently do anything in the way of parts and his name is always potent box-office for the younger set, the most important single segment of our audience."
HOLLYWOOD REPORTER

Universal-International

"An energetic and sharply-paced melodrama, in which the emphasis is mainly on straightforward and sometimes unnecessarily violent action. Performances are standard, with Arthur Kennedy rather overplaying the part of the good-natured cynical charmer and Tony Curtis presenting a decidedly modern appearance as the misunderstood Ben."

MONTHLY FILM BULLETIN

TRAPEZE

U.S.A. 1956 – RUNNING TIME: 106 MINUTES
HECHT-LANCASTER PRODUCTIONS

		CAST	
DIRECTOR:	CAROL REED		
PRODUCER:	JAMES HILL		
SCREENPLAY:	JAMES R. WEBB	BURT LANCASTER	MIKE RIBBLE
ART DIRECTION:	RINO MONDELLINI	TONY CURTIS	TINO ORSINI
DIRECTOR OF PHOTOGRAPHY:	ROBERT KRASKER	GINA LOLLOBRIGIDA	LOLA
EDITOR:	BERT BATES	KATY JURADO	ROSA
MUSIC:	MALCOLM ARNOLD	THOMAS GOMEZ	BOUGLIONE
COSTUMES:	FRANK SALVI AND	JOHNNY PULEO	MAX
	GLADYS DE SEGONZAC	MINOR WATSON	JOHN RINGLING-NORTH
		GERARD LANDRY	CHIKKI
		J.P. KERRIEN	OTTO
		SIDNEY JAMES	SNAKE MAN
		GABRIELLE FONTEN	OLD WOMAN

'Trapeze' realised the long standing ambition of former acrobat Burt Lancaster to make a circus film. The one million pound production was filmed entirely in Paris at the Cirque d'Hiver and the Billancourt studios. Curtis received a reputed salary of one hundred and fifty thousand dollars and, at Lancaster's request, trained with Eddie Ward from Ringling Brothers to ensure that the amount of doubling was kept to a minimum. Some of the aerial stunts were so dangerous that even the doubles were required to have doubles. The film was a major box-office success, taking seven and a half million dollars in America during 1956. At the Berlin Film Festival of that year Lancaster was awarded 'Best Actor' for his performance.

Tino Orsini, a brash young American acrobat, arrives at the Cirque Bouglione. He seeks out Mike Ribble, his father's former partner, and attempts to persuade him to become his trainer and mentor. In particular he wants Mike to teach him the dangerous aerial triple somersault. Mike, crippled from a fall, agrees to be his catcher and teach him the movement.

Tino learns quickly and a successful partnership begins to develop. Lola, a beautiful but scheming tumbler, attempts to break into the act using her feminine wiles on Tino. There are tensions in the relationship before Lola realises that she really loves Mike. Much to Mike's disgust she continues to use Tino to further her career. He determines to expose her exploitation of Tino but resists when he realises that he loves Lola too. When Tino learns of their love he refuses to perform with Mike.

Mike is well aware of Tino's dependence on him to perform the triple somersault. When an American impresario comes to the circus talent-scouting Mike substitutes for Tino's catcher and, despite their mutual dislike, Tino manages a perfect triple. Tino has achieved his ambition and seems set for a successful circus career. He can forgive Mike who quietly slips away with Lola leaving Tino in the limelight.

"As the young man who comes to Paris to learn the 'triple' – a difficult manoeuvre performed in the past by six men only – Tony Curtis is most engaging. His crew-cut voice has an eager note contrasting splendidly with the ursine growl of Burt Lancaster."

SUNDAY TIMES

"Curtis has had to overcome the fact that he is a very handsome young man. He has done it so that his appearance is now secondary to a talent and vitality that mark him as one of the most important young stars."

HOLLYWOOD REPORTER

Burt Lancaster and Gina Lollobrigida

Hecht-Lancaster Productions

MISTER CORY

U.S.A. 1956 – RUNNING TIME: 92 MINUTES
UNIVERSAL-INTERNATIONAL

DIRECTOR:	BLAKE EDWARDS	**CAST**
PRODUCER:	ROBERT ARTHUR	
SCREENPLAY:	BLAKE EDWARDS FROM A STORY	TONY CURTIS — MISTER CORY
	BY LEO ROSTEN	MARTHA HYER — ABBY VOLLARD
ART DIRECTION:	ALEXANDER GOLITZEN AND	CHARLES BICKFORD — BILOXI
	ERIC ORBOM	KATHRYN GRANT — JEN VOLLARD
DIRECTOR OF PHOTOGRAPHY:	RUSSELL METTY	WILLIAM REYNOLDS — ALEX WYNCOTT
EDITOR:	EDWARD CURTISS	HENRY DANIELL — EARNSHAW
SOUND:	LESLIE I. CAREY AND	RUSS MORGAN — RUBY MATROBE
	CORSON JOWETT	WILLIS BOUCHEY — MR VOLLARD
PRODUCTION MANAGER:	SERGEI PETSCHNIKOFF	LOUISE LORIMER — MRS VOLLARD
MUSIC:	JOSEPH GERSHENSON	JOAN BANKS — LOLA
COSTUMES:	BILL THOMAS	

'Mister Cory' was an early film as director for Blake Edwards who would later work with Curtis several times. A former actor, Edwards had been a script-writer for several years, often in tandem with director Richard Quine. He made his debut as a director in 1955 with 'Bring Your Smile Along' and 'Mister Cory' was one of many light entertainments he was responsible for before finding his cinematic feet. In the film Curtis winds up with Jen Vollard played by Kathryn Grant who retired from the screen a few years later when she became Bing Crosby's wife.

'Mister' Cory is an ambitious young gambler from the slums of Chicago who seeks wealth and social position. He finds work as a dishwasher at a country club where he meets heiress Abby Vollard, her sister Jen and professional gambler Jeremiah Caldwell, known as Biloxi.

Cory pursues Abby who is only interested in him as a plaything; she intends to marry Alex Wyncott, her social equal. Jen however is very interested in Cory although initially he remains immune to her charms. When Abby discovers that he is merely a dishwasher Cory leaves the resort. Over the next year Cory amasses some money whilst working in the Texas oilfields. In Reno he meets Biloxi again and the two form a partnership. Eventually Cory is offered the job as manager of the Dolphin casino in Chicago. He is immensely successful and again attracts the attentions of Abby who is now engaged to Alex. Alex learns about Cory and tries to put him in his place but to no avail. The Dolphin's owner, Ruby Matrobe, is furious at Alex's humiliation as his father is one of the most influential people in Chicago and has already closed two of his operations. Matrobe advises Cory to leave town but Alex arrives threatening to kill Cory. Alex only wounds Cory but Matrobe senses an opportunity to blackmail Alex's father into leaving his business activities unharmed. However, Cory is impressed by the strength of Alex's feelings towards Abby and promises he will swear that he injured himself cleaning his guns.

Cory decides on a fresh start and, as he boards a plane leaving Chicago, he is joined by Jen.

"Curtis can carry this kind of role perfectly. He is one of the few young stars of major value who has that contained recklessness, insouciance and bubbling good humour that regrettably has been lost in the current substitution of soiled T-shirts for the Byronic Collar. Curtis can play the earthy parts too, but he is not limited."

HOLLYWOOD REPORTER

"Curtis gives the title role a good personality ride and pleases."

VARIETY

William Reynolds and Martha Hyer

Universal-International

THE MIDNIGHT STORY

UK: APPOINTMENT WITH A SHADOW

U.S.A. 1957 – RUNNING TIME: 90 MINUTES
UNIVERSAL-INTERNATIONAL

		CAST	
DIRECTOR:	JOSEPH PEVNEY		
PRODUCER:	ROBERT ARTHUR		
SCREENPLAY:	JOHN ROBINSON AND	**TONY CURTIS**	JOE MARTINI
	EDWIN BLUM	**MARISA PAVAN**	ANNA MALATESTA
ART DIRECTION:	ALEXANDER GOLITZEN AND	**GILBERT ROLAND**	SYLVIO MALATESTA
	ERIC ORBOM	**PEGGY MALEY**	VEDA PINELLI
DIRECTOR OF PHOTOGRAPHY:	RUSSELL METTY	**JAY C. FLIPPEN**	SGT. JACK GILLEN
EDITOR:	TED J. KENT	**ARGENTINA BRUNETTI**	MAMA MALATESTA
SOUND:	LESLEY I. CAREY AND	**TED DE CORSIA**	LT. KILRAIN
	FRANK H. WILKINSON	**RICHARD MONDA**	PEANUTS MALATESTA
MUSIC:	JOSEPH GERSHENSON	**KATHLEEN FREEMAN**	ROSA CUNEO
COSTUMES:	BILL THOMAS		

Curtis usually managed to appear in the better films of prolific director Joseph Pevney. 'The Midnight Story', their third and final collaboration, is no exception. Pevney, a former actor from New York, had first worked with Curtis on 'Flesh and Fury' and had extracted a promising suggestion of his acting potential. 'The Midnight Story' is a sign of just how much Curtis had improved and developed that potential in the intervening five years. Curtis gives a convincing and mature performance in this atmospheric thriller.

San Francisco. Father Tomasino, a beloved figure in his dockside parish, is brutally murdered. Traffic policeman Joe Martini is particularly shocked by the murder and asks for a transfer to the homicide department. When his request is denied he leaves the force to carry out a private investigation.

At the funeral Joe observes Sylvio Malateste who is so upset that he scrapes Rosary beads across his hands until they bleed. Joe manages to obtain work at Sylvio's seafood restaurant and is soon befriended by the Malateste family who invite him to board with them. Joe is relieved to discover that Sylvio was playing pool with a friend when the murder was committed. Joe falls in love with Sylvio's cousin Anna and their marriage is announced. During the engagement celebrations Joe learns that Sylvio's alibi was false. Joe is reluctant to believe that Sylvio was the murderer but his love for the priest drives him on to discover the truth.

Anna learns that Joe is a former policeman and confesses to Sylvio that she is concerned as to why he has left the force. Sylvio confronts Joe and demands the gun that he carries. Joe claims that he intends to kill a blackmailer he believes to have murdered Tomasino. Sylvio begs Joe to pay the man off instead of killing him. He tells Joe that he once killed a girl in Naples and has been consumed with guilt ever since. Joe asks why he had never confessed his crime to Father Tomasino. Sylvio attacks him with a knife and tries to escape but runs into the path of a truck. As he lies dying in hospital Sylvio confesses that Tomasino had told him to go to the police but that he didn't want to besmirch the family name. His torment had caused him to murder Tomasino.

Argentina Brunetti and Gilbert Roland   Universal-International

"With each successive film Tony Curtis proves again that he must no longer be regarded as a mere 'pretty boy' but as a serious actor. With the help of the highly reliable Gilbert Roland as partner he puts in here a performance of considerable dramatic depth."

TODAY'S CINEMA

"The acting – particularly of Tony Curtis as the priest's avenger and Gilbert Roland as the murderer – is accomplished and the whole production evidences a purposeful sincerity."

MONTHLY FILM BULLETIN

SWEET SMELL OF SUCCESS

U.S.A. 1957 – RUNNING TIME: 93 MINUTES
HECHT-HILL-LANCASTER PRODUCTIONS

		CAST	
DIRECTOR:	ALEXANDER MACKENDRICK		
PRODUCER:	JAMES HILL		
EXECUTIVE PRODUCER:	HAROLD HECHT	BURT LANCASTER	J.J. HUNSECKER
SCREENPLAY:	CLIFFORD ODETS AND	TONY CURTIS	SIDNEY FALCO
	ERNEST LEHMAN	SUSAN HARRISON	SUSAN HUNSECKER
ART DIRECTION:	EDWARD CARRERE	MARTY MILNER	STEVE DALLAS
DIRECTOR OF PHOTOGRAPHY:	JAMES WONG HOWE	SAM LEVENE	FRANK D'ANGELO
EDITOR:	ALAN CROSLAND JNR.	BARBARA NICHOLS	RITA
SOUND:	JACK SOLOMON	JEFF DONNELL	SALLY
MUSIC:	ELMER BERNSTEIN	JOSEPH LEON	ROBARD
		EDITH ATWATER	MARY
		EMILE MEYER	HARRY KELLO
		JOE FRISCO	HERBIE TEMPLE

'Sweet Smell of Success' finally laid to rest any doubts regarding Tony Curtis's ability as an actor. His venal, conniving press agent is a scrupulously well observed portrait of corruptibility. Burt Lancaster had been impressed by Curtis's commitment to 'Trapeze' and also sensed an ambitious actor hemmed in by his image as a swashbuckling man of action, an image that might well have hampered Lancaster's own career a decade before. Thus he decided to take a chance on Curtis when casting 'Sweet Smell of Success' for his own company.

The film was not a box-office success in 1957 but the brittle dialogue of the script, the quality of the performances and the remarkable direction of Britisher Alexander Mackendrick have earned it a status as a classic.

J.J. Hunsecker of 'The Globe' is the most powerful columnist in New York; a ruthless, calculating man who cares for no-one except his 19 year-old sister Susie. Sidney Falco is a young, unscrupulous press agent dependent on the likes of Hunsecker to publicise his clients. For five days Hunsecker has cut Falco from his column as a punishment. Falco was entrusted to break-up the romance between Susie and guitar-player Steve Dallas, a man Hunsecker deems unworthy of his sister. Falco has failed and now the couple are planning marriage.

With Hunsecker's complicity Falco works on a plan to end the romance permanently. A smear is printed in a rival column that Dallas is both a Communist and involved in drugs; he is immediately sacked by the Elysian nightclub. Falco persuades Hunsecker to intervene and arrange Dallas's reinstatement, aware that the musician's pride will not allow him to accept the favour.

Meeting during rehearsals for Hunsecker's TV show 'It's a Wonderful World', Falco goads Dallas into rejecting Hunsecker's help. Aware of the scheming around him Dallas vilifies Hunsecker as a national disgrace. Susie promises never to see Dallas again. However Hunsecker has been personally insulted and exacts his revenge. Falco frames Dallas on a drugs charge and is rewarded with the assurance that he will.write Hunsecker's column while J.J. is on holiday.

Triumphant, Falco is summoned to Hunsecker's apartment. J.J. is not to be seen but Susie is and, to undermine Falco's newfound status with her brother, she threatens suicide. When J.J. arrives he finds Falco and Susie in a seemingly compromising situation and is outraged. He frees Dallas and implicates Falco in the drugs case. Falco is arrested. Meanwhile Susie finally stands up for herself and leaves home for Dallas. J.J. has been defeated.

Burt Lancaster   Hecht-Hill-Lancaster Productions

"Tony Curtis astonishingly persuasive as a sickening agent prepared to slide through any slime for a fast dollar."

SUNDAY EXPRESS

"Curtis, foxy eyes set in a little-boy face, has never done anything better. His performance is something to goggle at."

DAILY HERALD

"And the playing - particularly that of Tony Curtis - has an attack and authority that drive a melodramatic plot at a pell-mell pace."

EVENING STANDARD

THE VIKINGS

U.S.A. 1958 – RUNNING TIME: 114 MINUTES
BRYNA PRODUCTION

		CAST	
DIRECTOR:	RICHARD FLEISCHER		
PRODUCER:	JERRY BRESLER		
SCREENPLAY:	CALDER WILLINGHAM, ADAPTED BY	KIRK DOUGLAS	EINAR
	DALE WASSERMAN FROM THE NOVEL	TONY CURTIS	ERIC
	'THE VIKING' BY EDISON MARSHALL	ERNEST BORGNINE	RAGNAR
ART DIRECTION:	HARPER GOFF	JANET LEIGH	MORGANA
DIRECTOR OF PHOTOGRAPHY:	JACK CARDIFF	JAMES DONALD	EGBERT
EDITOR:	ELMO WILLIAMS	ALEXANDER KNOX	FATHER GODWIN
SOUND:	JO DE BRETAGNE	FRANK THRING	AELLA
MUSIC:	MARIO NASCIMBENE	MAXINE AUDLEY	ENID
NARRATOR:	ORSON WELLES	EILEEN WAY	KITALA
		EDRIC CONNOR	SANDPIPER
		DANDY NICHOLS	BRIDGET
		PER BUCHHIJ	BJORN
		ALMUT BERG	PIGTAILS

A thundering, blood-and-guts adventure 'The Vikings' was based on a bestselling novel of 1951. The producer and director began scouting for locations in September 1956 eventually choosing areas in France and Norway. To reach one location at Hardangerfjord involved the use of a car, a ferry and a boat ride. In an interview the film's producer, Jerry Bresler, said; "It's been an absolute nightmare. In Norway we hired a white horse from a local stables. When the owner heard it was for Kirk Douglas he doubled the price. I refused to pay so he cut off the whole water supply to the unit." Bresler also found that the wolves they had hired were too ferocious to set loose on expensive Hollywood stars; "Now we have to use Alsatians. We're going to paint them black, grease their coats and dub wolf howls on the soundtrack."

'The Vikings' was filmed on a budget of three and a half million dollars for Kirk Douglas's Bryna Productions. The star received no salary but he was entitled to 60% of the profits. In 1958 the film was number five at the American box-office taking seven million dollars and it was estimated that Douglas would earn in excess of two million dollars.

The 9th Century. England is a country of fragmented kingdoms subject to swift and brutal Viking raids. During one raid Viking King Ragnar slays the English King and rapes Queen Enid. The crown passes to the wastrel Aella but the Queen is aware that the rightful heir is her unborn child. When she gives birth to a son called Eric she enlists the aid of Father Godwin and the boy is sent on a pilgrim ship to Rome. He wears the pommelstone of Northumbria's Sword Requitur signifying his right to the throne. During the journey the ship is seized by the Vikings and Eric grows up a slave.

Twenty years later Aella is ensconced on the throne of Northumbria and plans to wed Morgana, daughter of the King of Wales, thus uniting the two kingdoms. His kinsman Egbert has designs on the throne and flees England to join forces with Ragnar. Whilst falconing with Ragnar's son Einar, he encounters Eric who is taunted by Einar and sets his falcon on him, causing him to lose an eye. Eric is tortured but survives and Egbert, who has recognised the pommelstone, claims him as his slave.

Einar sets sail and captures Morgana but Eric rescues her and heads for England. Ragnar follows them but his ship is wrecked and Aella orders his execution in a pit of wolves. Eric gives Ragnar a sword so that he may die like a warrior and is rewarded for his concern by having his left hand

Kirk Douglas   Bryna Productions

severed. He is set adrift in a small craft and returns to put aside his differences with Einar and sail to England. Aella is defeated and put to death. Eric is recognised as the heir and revealed as Einar's half brother but Einar insists that they duel to resolve their love for Morgana. Eric is victorious but ensures that Einar receives a full Viking funeral.

"The Vikings is, in fact, a bloodthirsty fandango of smash, kick, gouge and punch which would be lamentable to watch were it not for one thing - it is played throughout with a tongue-in-cheek sense of serio-comedy that makes you laugh out loud in the moments when you might be shuddering with horror. It is rough, riotous and wholly enjoyable."

DAILY EXPRESS

THE DEFIANT ONES

U.S.A. 1958 – RUNNING TIME: 96 MINUTES
LOMITAS-CURTLEIGH PRODUCTION

		CAST	
DIRECTOR:	STANLEY KRAMER		
PRODUCER:	STANLEY KRAMER		
SCREENPLAY:	NATHAN E. DOUGLAS AND	TONY CURTIS	JOHN 'JOKER' JACKSON
	HAROLD JACOB SMITH	SIDNEY POITIER	NOAH CULLEN
ART DIRECTION:	RUDOLPH STERNAD	CARA WILLIAMS	THE WOMAN
DIRECTOR OF PHOTOGRAPHY:	SAM LEAVITT	THEODORE BIKEL	SHERIFF MAX MULLER
EDITOR:	FREDERIC KNUDTSON	CHARLES MCGRAW	FRANK GIBBONS
MUSIC:	ERNEST GOLD	LON CHANEY JR	BIG SAM
COSTUMES:	JOE KING	KING DONOVAN	SOLLY
		CLAUDE AKINS	MAC
		LAWRENCE DOBKIN	EDITOR
		WHIT BISSELL	LOU GANS

Producer-director Stanley Kramer has a long career of tackling sensitive and topical issues in the films he has made. Curtis was so convinced of the worth of 'The Defiant Ones' that his company, Curtleigh, was involved in the struggle to raise the one million dollar budget. He wore a false nose for his part, fearful that his good looks might intrude on reactions to his bigoted character.

The film was nominated for several Academy Awards including the Best Film of 1958. Curtis and Poitier both received nominations as Best Actor although David Niven was announced the winner for 'Separate Tables'. The film did win two Oscars; one for Sam Leavitt's cinematography and a further one for the screenplay by Nathan E. Douglas and Harold Jacob Smith. Douglas was a pseudonym for blacklisted actor Nedrick Young who had taken the fifth amendment when questioned by the House of Un-American Activities in 1953.

The film received many honours from around the world; the New York Film Critics voted it 'Best Film', the Berlin Film Festival awarded Poitier 'Best Actor', the British Academy gave it the United Nations Award and named Poitier as 'Best Foreign Actor'.

John Jackson and Noah Cullen, prisoners in a chain gang, manage to escape when a truck crashes. Bound together by a chain there is a bitter enmity between the vicious Jackson and the soulful negro. They take flight through swampland followed closely by Sheriff Max Muller who leads a posse of state troopers and civilians. The posse is aided by bloodhounds and dobermans. Police captain Gibbons wants the prisoners dead or alive whilst Muller advocates caution and keeps the dogs under leash.

The fugitives are obliged to look after each other and, whilst crossing a swollen river, Jackson saves Cullen as he struggles in the raging water. Eventually they reach a settlement and break into a store seeking food and tools. However, they are detected and an angry crowd threatens to lynch them. They are tied to a post but later freed by Big Sam whose wrist shows the scars of manacles.

The frustration and despair felt by the men leads to a fight which is stopped by a young boy who holds them at bay with his rifle. His mother feeds them and provides them with a hammer and chisel to break their chain. She nurses Jackson who has become feverish from his wounds. Next morning she is prepared to travel on with Jackson in her car and directs Cullen to a safe route through the swamps. When she later admits sending Cullen to an area of quicksand Jackson abandons her and catches up with Cullen. With the posse fast approaching the two men try to board a freight train but fail. Capture now certain Cullen sits singing, cradling Jackson in his arms.

Sidney Poitier   Lomitas-Curtleigh Productions

"In each picture recently Tony Curtis has been proving that his bobbysox past is a long way behind him. And with 'The Defiant Ones' he achieves his best yet: a performance of corrosive and devastating power."

EVENING STANDARD

KINGS GO FORTH

U.S.A. 1958 – RUNNING TIME: 109 MINUTES
UNITED ARTISTS

DIRECTOR:	DELMER DAVES	
PRODUCER:	FRANK ROSS	
ASSOCIATE PRODUCER:	RICHARD ROSS	
SCREENPLAY:	MERLE MILLER FROM THE NOVEL	
	BY JOE DAVID BROWN	
ART DIRECTION:	FERNANDO CARRERE	
DIRECTOR OF PHOTOGRAPHY:	DANIEL FAPP	
EDITOR:	WILLIAM B. MURPHY	
PRODUCTION MANAGER:	RICHARD MCWHORTER	
MUSIC:	ELMER BERNSTEIN	
COSTUMES:	LEA RHODES	

CAST

FRANK SINATRA	SAM LOGGINS
TONY CURTIS	BRITT HARRIS
NATALIE WOOD	MONIQUE BLAIR
LEORA DANA	MRS BLAIR
KARL SWENSON	COLONEL
ANNE CODEE	MADAME BRIEUX
EDWARD RYDER	CORP. LINDSAY
JACKIE BERTHE	JEAN FRANCOIS
MARIE ISNARD	OLD FRENCHWOMAN

In a rather overheated drama the central issue of a mixed-race parentage emerges as much ado about nothing. However, 'Kings Go Forth' did afford Curtis an opportunity to work with Frank Sinatra and, for a while, he was associated with the famous Rat Pack of Sinatra's cronies.

The film's world premiere was held on June 14th, 1958 in Monte Carlo under the patronge of the Prince and Princess Rainier, the former Grace Kelly. Frank Sinatra was on hand for a concert to benefit the United Nations fund for refugees which raised twelve thousand dollars.

1944. In southern France the American 7th Army are pushing back the remaining pockets of German resistance to the Allied advance. Among the newest reinforcements is Britt Harris who is attached as a radio operator to Sam Loggins.

During his leave Sam meets Monique Blair, an American girl living with her widowed mother. Monique seems reluctant to let their relationship develop but Sam befriends Mrs Blair and becomes a frequent visitor to their villa. Sam asks Monique to marry him but she refuses, revealing that she is the child of a mixed marriage; her father was a negro. Sam ponders this and concludes that his love for Monique can overcome any obstacle. He returns to the villa and takes Monique to Nice for the evening. In Nice they meet Britt and, for Monique, it is love at first sight. Initially Sam is jealous but resigns himself to losing her and, on Monique's behalf, he explains to Britt about her father. Britt seems indifferent to the news and later announces their marriage, asking Sam to act as best man.

Sam and Britt volunteer for a dangerous mission to penetrate the German lines. A few hours before going into combat Sam discovers that Britt had received his marriage application three weeks previously and done nothing about it. At the Blair villa Britt admits that he never intended to marry Monique. Monique tries to drown herself but is consoled by Sam who vows to kill Britt. However, during their raid on German emplacements Britt is shot dead by a sniper's bullet. Sam is wounded and loses an arm.

After the war Sam returns to Monique's village. Her mother is dead and she has turned the villa into a school for war orphans.

Frank Sinatra   United Artists

"By sheer insouciance Curtis makes this intriguing and repulsive individual completely believable because each of us recognizes in him some of the human enigmas encountered in life. Sinatra is superb as a man with great capacities of devotion and little self conceit. Curtis is equally fine as the reckless show-off who arouses pity by his very shallowness."

HOLLYWOOD REPORTER

"Curtis has had experience acting the heel, and he does a repeat, though his is a tough character to swallow. He's best when acting the charm boy."

VARIETY

THE PERFECT FURLOUGH

UK: STRICTLY FOR PLEASURE

U.S.A. 1958 – RUNNING TIME: 93 MINUTES
UNIVERSAL-INTERNATIONAL

		CAST	
DIRECTOR:	BLAKE EDWARDS		
PRODUCER:	ROBERT ARTHUR		
SCREENPLAY:	STANLEY SHAPIRO	TONY CURTIS	PAUL HODGES
ART DIRECTION:	ALEXANDER GOLITZEN	JANET LEIGH	VICKI LOREN
DIRECTOR OF PHOTOGRAPHY:	PHILIP LATHROP	KEENAN WYNN	HARVEY FRANKLIN
EDITOR:	MILTON CARRUTH	LINDA CRISTAL	SANDRA ROCA
SOUND:	LESLIE I. CAREY AND	ELAINE STRITCH	LIZ BAKER
	FRANK WILKINSON	MARCEL DALIO	HENRI
PRODUCTION MANAGER:	FOSTER THOMPSON	LES TREMAYNE	COLONEL LELAND
MUSIC:	FRANK SKINNER	JAY NOVELLO	RENE
COSTUMES:	BILL THOMAS	KING DONOVAN	MAJOR COLLINS
		FRANKIE DARRO	PATIENT
		TROY DONAHUE	SGT. NICKLES

A diverting, escapist comedy 'The Perfect Furlough' employed the talents of Blake Edwards, latterly best known for the Pink Panther escapades, and scriptwriter Stanley Shapiro who provided some of the best later vehicles for Cary Grant. The film was fairly and squarely aimed at the youth market and had an immensely successful preview before a college audience at Westwood Village in Los Angeles. One eager, but surely hyperbolic, publicist guaranteed that he had counted 287 laughs during the screening.

As a morale booster at an isolated polar Army Base psychologist Vicki Loren suggests that one of the men be granted a perfect furlough to spend as he desires. By hook and by crook the winner is corporal Paul Hodges who chooses to spend the leave in Paris with film star Sandra Roca. Sandra is charmed into the idea by her manager Henry Franklin.

In Paris Paul finds his style cramped by the constant presence of two MPs and chaperone Vicki. After various abortive attempts to spend time alone with Sandra he finally succeeds and the two go for a picnic. Sandra admits that she is secretly married and the couple head straight back to the hotel. En route they stop for petrol at a vintner's and Sandra falls into a wine vat. Back at the hotel Vicki notices their dishevelled appearance and jumps to the obvious conclusions. Paul tries to reason with her and they return to the vintner where Vicki also falls into the wine vat, creating the same impression on their return to the hotel.

Sandra feels a cold coming on and summons a doctor who discovers that she is pregnant and assumes that Paul is the father. The Army hastily arranges a marriage. Vicki is heartbroken and plans to fly back to America but is ordered to stay when the Army receives an unfounded report that she is also pregnant by Paul. Sandra clears up the matter and Paul requests a return to his Arctic base. Vicki falsely claims that she really is an expectant mother so that she can keep Paul with her. He states that he will have their marriage annulled 'in about fifty or sixty years'.

Janet Leigh   Universal-International

"It should do well at the box-office for it co-stars Tony Curtis, now at his height as a ticket seller and Janet Leigh looking at once sweet and wholesome and sexy."

HOLLYWOOD REPORTER

"Curtis plays comedy well, playing it broadly and agreeably. Miss Leigh is the psychologist; this profession rarely yields such attractive practitioners.

VARIETY

SOME LIKE IT HOT

U.S.A. 1959 – RUNNING TIME: 120 MINUTES
ASHTON PRODUCTION-MIRISCH COMPANY PRESENTATION

		CAST	
DIRECTOR:	BILLY WILDER		
PRODUCER:	BILLY WILDER		
ASSOCIATE PRODUCERS:	DOANE HARRISON/	MARILYN MONROE	SUGAR KOWALCZYK
	I.A.L. DIAMOND	TONY CURTIS	JOE/JOSEPHINE
SCREENPLAY:	BILLY WILDER/I.A.L. DIAMOND	JACK LEMMON	JERRY/DAPHNE
	SUGGESTED BY A STORY BY	GEORGE RAFT	SPATS
	R. THOEREN AND M. LOGAN	JOE E. BROWN	OSGOOD FIELDING III
ART DIRECTION:	TED HAWORTH	PAT O'BRIEN	MULLIGAN
DIRECTOR OF PHOTOGRAPHY:	CHARLES LANG JR.	JOAN SHAWLEE	SWEET SUE
EDITOR:	ARTHUR SCHMIDT	NEHEMIAH PERSOFF	LITTLE BONAPARTE
SOUND:	FRED LAU	GEORGE STONE	TOOTHPICK CHARLIE
PRODUCTION COORDINATOR:	ALLEN K. WOOD	DAVE BARRY	BEINSTOCK
MUSIC:	ADOLPH DEUTSCH		
COSTUMES:	ORRY KELLY		
CHOREOGRAPHY:	WALLY GREEN		

Had Curtis made only this film he would have merited his place in the film history books. Billy Wilder's brilliant comedy was based on a German film in which two male musicians are forced to join an all-female band and was once considered as a script for Bob Hope and Danny Kaye. Later, Wilder wrote the role of Jerry/Daphne especially for Jack Lemmon after having seen the actor in 'Operation Mad Ball' (1957). Curtis was cast as Joe and Mitzi Gaynor would play Sugar. It was felt that Wilder needed a stronger box-office line-up and Lemmon was almost jettisoned in favour of Frank Sinatra. When the company was able to cast Marilyn Monroe as Sugar, Wilder was allowed to take a chance on the chemistry of Curtis and Lemmon.

Curtis has rarely been in better form than in his sole appearance for Wilder and the film reflects his ability to respond well to a talented director. Later he recalled; "Wilder gave us a lot of freedom. He got a female impersonator in to show Jack and I how to behave in drag: we were told if you let your arm go limp it takes away the muscle-bulge. With my part I kept Grace Kelly very much in mind. I decided I was going to be rather aloof and stylish: I wasn't going to be no easy lay who hit the sack for just anybody."

The film was number three at the American box-office in 1959, having accumulated seven million dollars, a figure that would eventually rise to fifteen million according to Lemmon in 1964. The film was nominated for several Academy Awards including 'Best Director', and 'Best Actor' for Lemmon. 1959 however was the year of 'Ben Hur' and 'Some Like It Hot' won only one award for costume design. The British Academy chose Lemmon as their 'Best Foreign Actor'.

Chicago, 1929. Musicians Joe and Jerry are employed at Mozarella's Funeral Parlour, a front for a speakeasy run by gangster Spats Columbo. Acting on information received from stoolpigeon 'Toothpick' Charlie, policeman Mulligan raids the establishment. Once again Joe and Jerry are penniless and unemployed. Booking agencies offer little hope of work. There is a desperate need for a sax player and a bow fiddler to join a band headed for Florida. The only catch is that the band is all-female. Joe and Jerry are to play one night at a dance and they head for 'Toothpick' Charlie's garage to collect a car. There they inadvertently witness the St. Valentine's Day Massacre as Spats and his gang take their vengeance. Fleeing the garage they decide to take the job in Florida.

Marilyn Monroe   Ashton-Mirisch Company Productions

Disguised as 'Josephine' and 'Daphne' the musicians join 'Sweet Sue and her Society Syncopators'. They also encounter the band's singer Sugar; a vulnerable, love-hungry blonde. At Miami Beach 'Daphne' catches the eye of oft-married millionaire Osgood Fielding III. 'Daphne' is persuaded to let the romance blossom whilst Joe assumes the persona of a millionaire and begins wooing Sugar. Eventually 'Daphne' becomes engaged to Osgood and Sugar is smitten by Joe whom she believes to be Shell Oil Jr.

A 'Friends of Italian Opera' celebration in Florida heralds a gangland convention and the arrival of Spats. Joe and Jerry are spotted and the chase is on again.However, Spats and his gang are killed by rival mobsters who in turn are arrested by Mulligan. Joe's disguise is revealed to Sugar who loves him regardless of the fact that he is neither a millionaire nor a woman. 'Daphne' explains to Osgood that he is a man but Osgood merely observes that 'nobody's perfect' and all four sail off into the horizon.

"Bristling with gags, zipping through a quick change artist's routine, shinning down drain pipes, plunging into foam baths, here comes a brand new and quite remarkable comic. But a well-known name. I will soften the shock no longer: it is Tony Curtis."

EVENING STANDARD

OPERATION PETTICOAT

U.S.A. 1959 – RUNNING TIME: 124 MINUTES
UNIVERSAL-INTERNATIONAL/GRANART PRODUCTION

DIRECTOR:	BLAKE EDWARDS	CAST
PRODUCER:	ROBERT ARTHUR	
EXECUTIVE PRODUCER:	EDWARD MUHL	CARY GRANT — ADMIRAL MATT SHERMAN
SCREENPLAY:	STANLEY SHAPIRO AND	TONY CURTIS — LT. NICK HOLDEN
	MAURICE RICHLIN FROM A STORY BY	JOAN O'BRIEN — LT. DOLORES CRANDALL
	PAUL KING AND JOSEPH STONE	DINA MERRILL — LT. BARBARA DURAN
ART DIRECTION:	ALEXANDER GOLITZEN AND	ARTHUR O'CONNELL — SAM TOSTIN
	ROBERT E. SMITH	GENE EVANS — MOLUMPHREY
DIRECTOR OF PHOTOGRAPHY:	RUSSELL HARLAN	RICHARD SARGENT — STOVALL
EDITOR:	TED J. KENT AND FRANK GROSS	VIRGINIA GREGG — MAJOR EDNA HAYWARD
SOUND:	LESLIE I. CAREY AND	ROBERT F. SIMON — CAPT. J. B. HENDERSON
	VERNON W. KRAMER	
PRODUCTION MANAGER:	LEW LEARY	
MUSIC:	DAVID ROSE	
COSTUMES:	BILL THOMAS	

Having carried off a devastating parody of Cary Grant in 'Some Like It Hot' Curtis jumped at his one chance to work with his idol and friend. Released slightly later than 'Some Like It Hot' the film was listed as the number three film at the American box-office in 1960, having amassed six million eight hundred thousand dollars. Curtis was then approaching his peak standing as a box-office attraction and 'Operation Petticoat' was one of three of his films in the top twenty successes of 1960. The script received an Academy Award nomination but lost to 'Pillow Talk' — also co-written by Stanley Shapiro.

In 1977 American television unveiled a remake of 'Operation Petticoat' with Curtis's daughter, Jamie Lee, as one of the Army nurses.

Former wartime submarine Sea Tiger is headed for the junkyard. Admiral Matt Sherman, once the captain of the vessel, makes a sentimental return to his command and, whilst reading his journal, relives his war memories.

Sherman had led the Sea Tiger from Manila to Darwin in Australia following a Japanese air attack which had left the craft badly damaged. Lieutenant Nick Holden arrives as a replacement officer. He is an opportunistic man for whom wartime rationing holds no meaning and is able to scrounge whatever Sherman requires to keep the Sea Tiger afloat. On one island stop Nick comes to the aid of a party of stranded Army nurses that include Barbara Duran and Dolores Crandall. Dolores is accident prone and inadvertently fires the sub's only torpedo, destroying a small Japanese truck. At Cebu Nick sets up a gambling operation exchanging chips for submarine parts. He also obtains white and red lead for an anti-corrosive undercoating which blend into a fetching shade of pink. When the Sea Tiger is abruptly called to join battle it is the most unconventional craft in the war-painted pink and with a passenger list that includes Army nurses and the families of Nick's Filipino gambling buddies. Unfortunately neither side in the hostilities has a record of a pink submarine and when Sherman surfaces to greet an American destroyer the Sea Tiger is fired upon. Nick comes to the rescue by sending the nurses' underwear through a torpedo tube and they are now welcomed with open arms by the Americans who escort them to Darwin.

Back in the present Sherman greets the captain who is to escort the Sea Tiger to the junkyard — Commander Nick Holden, now happily married to Barbara. When Sherman's wife arrives she crashes her station wagon into his staff car. Dolores is as accident prone as ever.

Cary Grant, Joan O'Brien and Dina Merrill   Universal-International/Granart Productions

"But see this film if only to savour the perfectly matched comedy duo of Grant and Curtis. And watch out for Tony Curtis: he's going to be that rarest and most precious of beings, a great light actor.

I thought that Tony Curtis couldn't be any funnier than he was in 'Some Like It Hot' but here his impudence is even cooler, his self-assurance even more devastating."

DAILY EXPRESS

WHO WAS THAT LADY?

U.S.A. 1959 – RUNNING TIME: 114 MINUTES
COLUMBIA-ANSARK-GEORGE SIDNEY PRODUCTION

		CAST	
DIRECTOR:	GEORGE SIDNEY		
PRODUCER:	NORMAN KRASNA		
SCREENPLAY:	NORMAN KRASNA	TONY CURTIS	DAVID WILSON
	FROM HIS OWN PLAY	DEAN MARTIN	MICHAEL HANEY
	'WHO WAS THAT LADY I SAW YOU WITH?'	JANET LEIGH	ANN WILSON
ART DIRECTION	EDWARD HAWORTH	JAMES WHITMORE	HARRY POWELL
DIRECTOR OF PHOTOGRAPHY:	HARRY STRADLING	JOHN McINTIRE	BOB DOYLE
EDITOR:	VIOLA LAWRENCE	BARBARA NICHOLS	GLORIA COOGLE
SOUND:	JAMES FLASTER	LARRY KEATING	PARKER
MUSIC:	ANDRE PREVIN	LARRY STORCH	ORENOV
COSTUMES:	JEAN LOUIS	SIMON OAKLAND	BELKA
		JOI LANSING	FLORENCE COOGLE
		BARBARA HINES	GIRL

The final major appearance together of Curtis and Janet Leigh, 'Who Was That Lady?' had opened on Broadway in March 1958 with Peter Lind Hayes, Mary Healy and Ray Walston in the star roles. Curtis and Martin had both injured themselves prior to filming and were banned from playing tennis for the duration of the production. However, it was Leigh who injured herself. One scene called for her to douse Curtis with a bucket of water, she subsequently slipped on the wet and fell on an iron grating sustaining cuts and bruises to her knees. The company was visited by Groucho Marx who was enlisted to make a trailer for the film which wound up at number nineteen in the list of box-office hits in 1960, taking three million dollars.

David Wilson, a chemistry professor, is caught kissing a pretty student by his indignant wife Ann who claims she is leaving for Reno. David contacts his friend TV writer Mike Harvey to help extricate him from the mess. With the help of Schultz, a prop man at CBS, Mike concocts a story that they are FBI agents investigating secret academic projects and that the kissing was only in the line of duty. Ann is convinced by their act and forgives David.

Next day Schultz reports the story to two genuine FBI agents, Powell and Doyle. That evening David and Ann plan a reconciliation dinner but Mike uses their new-found profession to force David on a double date, claiming they are meeting foreign agents. Ann finds that David has left his gun behind and rushes after him. She bumps into Powell and explains her concern to him on the way to the restaurant. In the Lee Wong restaurant Ann overhears one of David's dinner companions saying 'get rid of 'em' and assumes the worst. She creates a disturbance during which Powell is wounded by a gun shot. David and Mike hit the headlines and are somehow hailed as heroes. They are visited by Parker of the CIA who believes them to be genuine and enlists their help to uncover the activities of foreign agents Orenov, Belka and Glinka. They receive a call from Belka to arrange a meeting which is obviously a trap but the CIA and FBI urge them to attend with their protection.

At the Empire State Building Mike is knocked out, Ann is chloroformed and David receives sodium pentothal. Under the drug David tells the truth about the FBI hoax. The foreign agents leave in disgust as does Ann who comes to first. When David and Mike awake they think they are on board a foreign submarine and, deciding to sacrifice themselves for the good of the country, turn on all the valves in sight —almost destroying the famous New York landmark and drowning. Powell saves them and even Ann finds that she can forgive David.

Dean Martin and Janet Leigh   Columbia-Ansark-George Sidney Productions

"Tony Curtis and Dean Martin make a superb comedy team in Columbia's 'Who Was That Lady?' Their pleasant personalities and buoyant sense of fun are ample compensations for the weaknesses of the farce situations."

DAILY WORKER

"So long as it doesn't happen too often there is nothing more cheering in the cinema than a film which is palpably, madly, wittily, mercilessly and deliberately absurd. 'Who Was That Lady?' fits the description."

SUNDAY EXPRESS

THE RAT RACE

U.S.A. 1960 - RUNNING TIME: 105 MINUTES
PERLBERG-SEATON PRODUCTION

		CAST	
DIRECTOR:	ROBERT MULLIGAN		
PRODUCERS:	WILLIAM PERLBERG AND		
	GEORGE SEATON	TONY CURTIS	PETE HAMMOND JR.
SCREENPLAY:	GARSON KANIN	DEBBIE REYNOLDS	PEGGY BROWN
	FROM HIS OWN PLAY	JACK OAKIE	MAC
ART DIRECTION:	HAL PEREIRA AND	KAY MEDFORD	SODA
	TAMBI LARSEN	DON RICKLES	NELLIE
DIRECTOR OF PHOTOGRAPHY:	ROBERT BURKS	JOE BUSHKIN	FRANKIE
EDITOR:	ALMA MACRORIE	SAM BUKERA	CARL
SOUND:	HUGO GRENZBACH AND	GERRY MULLIGAN	GERRY
	WINSTON LEVERETT		
MUSIC:	ELMER BERNSTEIN		

'The Rat Race' was completed in forty-six shooting days on locations in New York and Milwaukee and on sound stages in Hollywood. Curtis mastered the saxophone and the flute for his role which included two weeks of rehearsals with Debbie Reynolds prior to filming. Obviously a dedicated actor he still liked to display the rewards of his labours and would ride to work in his twenty-six thousand dollar Rolls Royce.

Curtis and Reynolds worked well together and at the party to mark the completion of filming she gave him an art set and he gave her a modern painting of a trumpeter. Director Robert Mulligan said; "It was my second picture, and it gave me a chance to learn. I had a good time working with Debbie and Tony. They were both pros, and there was never any of that star crazy stuff." The film was another success and earned three million, four hundred thousand dollars in 1960.

Aspiring musician Pete Hammond Jnr. arrives in New York from Milwaukee seeking fame and fortune. He meets Mac, a sympathetic bartender, who suggests a boarding house where he might find cheap lodgings. Soda, the landlady, has a spare room as she is about to evict her tenant Peggy Brown for non-payment of rent. Pete feels sorry for Peggy and offers to share the room using a curtain as a dividing line.

Daily Pete learns more of Peggy's seedy life and how she works as a hostess in a dance hall run by a thug named Nellie. Success does not come as easily as he expected and Pete's naive impressionability lays him open to the wiles of his older colleagues who steal his instruments. He is given a chance to join a band on a South American cruise. Peggy secures a loan from Nellie to enable him to purchase new instruments and he sets sail.

During Pete's absence Nellie tries to force Peggy into 'entertaining' his clients as a repayment for his generosity. She refuses and leaves the club. When Pete returns to New York Nellie greets him demanding full re-payment of his $600 loan. There is a fight but Pete hands over his earnings and his instruments to clear the debt.

Peggy feels she has let Pete down and is determined to leave New York. Pete is touched by her faithfulness during his absence and insists that they stay together. Neither has found fame or fortune but they are reconciled to the forthcoming struggle knowing that they have each other.

Perlberg-Seaton Production

"That their innocence does remain credible is due more to the playing of Tony Curtis (a delightful and increasingly subtle actor) and a newly acidulous Debbie Reynolds than to the writing."

FINANCIAL TIMES

SPARTACUS

U.S.A. 1960 – RUNNING TIME: 196 MINUTES
BRYNA PRODUCTION

		CAST	
DIRECTOR:	STANLEY KUBRICK		
PRODUCER:	EDWARD LEWIS		
EXECUTIVE PRODUCER:	KIRK DOUGLAS	KIRK DOUGLAS	SPARTACUS
SCREENPLAY:	DALTON TRUMBO FROM THE NOVEL	LAURENCE OLIVIER	CRASSUS
	BY HOWARD FAST	JEAN SIMMONS	VARINIA
ART DIRECTION:	ERIC ORBOM	TONY CURTIS	ANTONINUS
DIRECTOR OF PHOTOGRAPHY:	RUSSELL METTY AND	CHARLES LAUGHTON	GRACCHUS
	CLIFFORD STINE	PETER USTINOV	BATIATUS
EDITOR:	ROBERT LAWRENCE	JOHN GAVIN	JULIUS CAESAR
SOUND:	WALDON O. WATSON, JOE LAPIS,	NINA FOCH	HELENA GLABRUS
	MURRAY SPIVACK AND RONALD PIERCE	HERBERT LOM	TIGRANES
PRODUCTION MANAGER:	NORMAN DEMING	JOHN IRELAND	CRIXUS
MUSIC:	ALEX NORTH	JOHN DALL	GLABRUS
COSTUMES:	BILL THOMAS AND	WOODY STRODE	DRABA
	J.J. ARLINGTON VALLES		

One of the most intelligent epics produced by Hollywood in the 1960s, 'Spartacus' was a personal project of Curtis's friend Kirk Douglas. The film cost an estimated twelve million dollars and was in production for over a year, utilising one hundred major sets and employing eight thousand extras. Douglas hired director Stanley Kubrick to replace veteran Anthony Mann and further replaced German actress Sabina Bethman with Jean Simmons to ensure that the finished film fulfilled his dream. Curtis received a reputed half million dollar salary and special billing for his supporting role. One of his scenes, depicting a homosexual advance by Crassus to his character Antoninus, was deleted.

Spartacus earned around fifteen million dollars on its American release and won four Academy Awards for 'Costume Design', 'Cinematography', 'Art and Set Decoration', and for Peter Ustinov as 'Best Supporting Actor'.

73-72 B.C. The proud, rebellious Spartacus has lived all his adult life in servitude. One day he is purchased by the slave-dealer Batiatus to train at his gladiator school. As an incentive in their training the men are occasionally presented with a woman for their pleasure and thus Spartacus meets and falls in love with Varinia. The Roman general Crassus visits the school and demands an exhibition fight to the death. Spartacus is chosen to fight Draba. However Draba cannot bring himself to kill Spartacus and tries instead to attack the spectators, dying in the attempt. Spartacus is spared and marshals the growing discontent among the slaves to mount a successful revolt.

Spartacus and the slaves march south through Italy to reach the sea and their route to freedom. They are joined by many along the way including Antoninus, an educated slave, poet, juggler and magician, who has fled Rome and the unwanted attentions of Crassus. In initial skirmishes with the might of the Roman Empire Spartacus and his men triumph. In Rome wily old Senator Gracchus promises go-between Tigranes that if the slaves leave Italy by sea their escape will go unopposed. Crassus however, foresees military glory and the chance to attain absolute power; he pays the Silesian fleet to disperse, thus trapping Spartacus's army and forcing a battle. Crassus is victorious, thousands of slaves are killed and many captured — including Antoninus and Spartacus, although the latter is unknown to Crassus. Varinia and Spartacus's new-born son are taken to Crassus's household.

Crassus is now an absolute ruler; Gracchus is to be exiled and all the slaves are to be crucified.

Kirk Douglas   Bryna Productions

Spartacus kills Antoninus in a forced fight to the death and is himself to be crucified. As a final act Gracchus ensures the safe passage from Rome of Batiatus, Varinia and her child. On the Appian Way Varinia is able to show the dying Spartacus his son and promises that through the child the slaves revolt will never be forgotten.

"In some ways the most subtle performance in the film comes, very surprisingly, from Tony Curtis as the singing slave... This may not be the most spectacular of Curtis's screen roles but it is perhaps his cleverest portrayal all the same."

RECORD SHOW MIRROR

THE GREAT IMPOSTER

U.S.A. 1960 – RUNNING TIME: 112 MINUTES
UNIVERSAL-INTERNATIONAL

DIRECTOR:	ROBERT MULLIGAN	**CAST**
PRODUCER:	ROBERT ARTHUR	
SCREENPLAY:	LIAM O'BRIEN FROM THE BOOK	**TONY CURTIS** — FERDINAND WALDO DEMARA JR.
	BY ROBERT CRICHTON	**KARL MARLDEN** — FATHER DEVLIN
ART DIRECTION:	ALEXANDER GOLITZEN	**EDMOND O'BRIEN** — CAPT. GLOVER
	AND HARRY BUMSTEAD	**ARTHUR O'CONNELL** — CHANDLER
DIRECTOR OF PHOTOGRAPHY:	ROBERT BURKS	**GARY MERRILL** — DEMARA SR.
EDITOR:	FRED KNUDTSON	**JOAN BLACKMAN** — CATHY LACEY
SOUND:	WALDON O. WATSON	**RAYMOND MASSEY** — ABBOTT DONNER
	AND HENRY WILKINSON	**FRANK GORSHIN** — BARNEY
PRODUCTION MANAGER:	EDWARD DODDS	**SUE ANN LANGDON** — EULALIE
MUSIC:	HENRY MANCINI	**ROBERT MIDDLETON** — BROWN

The life story of Ferdinand Demara gave full rein to Curtis's versatility and he was keen to work again with director Robert Mulligan who had made 'The Rat Race'. Mulligan later said; "I wanted to do something absolutely outrageous. I remember that whole picture as being an absolute kick. It was such fun making that picture because the character was so crazy, and yet so real. I mean this guy had actually lived all those lives. I was intrigued by what this guy had said, that the reason he was successful was that most people don't know who they are. So if he presented himself as whoever he was — a doctor, a lawyer, a teacher, a priest, anything he wanted to be — if he did it with authority people accepted it."

Ferdinand Waldo Demara Jnr., using the pseudonym of Martin Goddard, is a highly respected teacher at a school in Haven Isle, Maine. One day the arrival of a State Trooper heralds his exposure as the 'Great Imposter'.

As a child Demara was a dreamer, eager for success but always seeking a short cut to enable him to achieve it. He enlists but is downcast when his poor educational qualifications prevent his acceptance into Officers' Training. He goes absent without leave, assumes the identity of a Dr. Robert Gilbert and gains a commission in the Marines, later faking his own suicide to prevent detection. Demara then returns home and his father persuades him to give himself up to the Military Police. At a railway station he is thrown in with a party of monks and is inspired to join their order posing as Brother Jerome. Unable to adjust to monastic life he leaves and is captured by the authorities and imprisoned in Disciplinary Barracks. He edits the prison newspaper and befriends the warden Ben Stone. On his discharge he assumes Stone's identity and is employed at a jail in the South where he succeeds in reforming the members of one of the toughest cell blocks. He is forced to move on and next becomes Dr. Mornay; a Canadian physician serving in the Navy. He falls in love with nurse Cathy Lacey but is unable to reveal the truth about his life of deception. In the war zone of Korea he distinguishes himself with a series of life-saving emergency operations and emerges a national hero. The resulting publicity exposes him again and he is discharged from the Naval Service.

He goes into hiding as a teacher but when the State Department searches for him they consult Maine State policeman Wilkerson who claims to have been the last man to have seen him. When Wilkerson is called in for questioning Demara's last great impersonation is discovered.

Gary Merrill   Universal-International

"Curtis is an authentic screen personality who, through hard work, has made himself an actor.
Demara's many facets afford Curtis a rare opportunity to demonstrate what movie acting is all
about – and Curtis shows that he has learned well.

SATURDAY REVIEW

"Mr Tony Curtis, by now one of Hollywood's most versatile and accomplished actors, works
wonders in holding the film together with his performance as Demara."

TIMES

THE OUTSIDER

U.S.A. 1961 – RUNNING TIME: 108 MINUTES
UNIVERSAL-INTERNATIONAL

DIRECTOR:	DELBERT MANN	CAST
PRODUCER:	SY BARTLETT	
SCREENPLAY:	STEWART STERN FROM THE BOOK	TONY CURTIS — IRA HAMILTON HAYES
	'THE HEROE OF IWO JIMA' BY	JAMES FRANCISCUS — JIM SORENSON
	WILLIAM BRADFORD HUIE	GREGORY WALCOTT — SERGEANT KILEY
ART DIRECTION:	ALEXANDER GOLITZEN AND	BRUCE BENNETT — MAJ. GEN. BRIDGES
	EDWARD S. HAWORTH	VIVIAN NATHAN — MRS NANCY HAYES
DIRECTOR OF PHOTOGRAPHY:	JOSEPH LA SHELLE	EDMUND HASHIM — JAY MORAGO
EDITOR:	MARJORIE FOWLER	PAUL COMI — SGT. BOYLE
SOUND:	WALDON O. WATSON AND	STANLEY ADAMS — NOOMIE, THE BARTENDER
	JOE LAPIS	WAYNE HEFFLEY — CORP. JOHNSON
PRODUCTION MANAGER:	MARSHALL GREEN	
MUSIC:	LEONARD ROSENMAN	

The true story of Ira Hayes gave Curtis one of his best dramatic roles but the film suffered from not possessing the courage of its convictions. He did not give a totally honest account of an ordinary man unable to live up to his own heroic image. The film romanticises the character and, in Britain, fifteen minutes were cut from the release print to minimise the scenes of alcoholism and unemployment faced by Hayes.

In real life Hayes was arrested fifty-one times for being drunk and disorderly, wound up on Chicago's skid row and was continually unemployed. He was found dead one morning having choked on his own vomit. As in 'The Defiant Ones' Curtis donned a false nose to aid his portrayal of the character.

Ira Hamilton Hayes, a young Pima Indian, is determined to serve his country during the Second World War and enlists in the Marines. He finds the rigorous training under Sergeant Kiley hard but is frequently helped by his company's top recruit Jim Sorenson.

One evening when Sorenson is drunk he picks a fight with Hayes and the two men end up friends. During the war they are among the six men who raise the American flag on the battlefield of Iwo Jima. Shortly afterwards Sorenson is killed by an enemy bomb.

Along with the two other survivors from the Iwo Jima flag-raising Hayes is recalled to Washington and given a hero's welcome. The three men are sent on an extensive war bond drive. Ira is still upset by his friend's death and disgusted by the hypocrisy surrounding their acts of heroism. He turns to drink and, although the Army tries to hide his condition from the public, he is disgraced and returns overseas to rejoin his outfit.

After the war he returns to the Pima reservation seeking to avoid the limelight. However, he soon senses that everyone will expect him to play the part of a 'hero' for the rest of his life and cannot accept the responsibility this places on him. Again he turns to drink and is arrested. He finds work as a cloakroom attendant but ends up in jail once more. Eventually he regains some self-respect and is able to attend the dedication ceremony for the Iwo Jima memorial.

"Curtis traces the career of this unfortunate young man with subtlety, perception and an astonishing depth of feeling. He bring the film alive and gives it a sense of urgency beyond either the script or the direction."

SATURDAY REVIEW

Universal-International

TARAS BULBA

U.S.A. 1962 – RUNNING TIME: 124 MINUTES
HAROLD HECHT-AVALA FILM

		CAST	
DIRECTOR:	J. LEE THOMPSON		
PRODUCER:	HAROLD HECHT		
SCREENPLAY:	WALDO SALT AND KARL TUNBERG	TONY CURTIS	ANDREI BULBA
	FROM THE NOVEL BY NICOLAI GOGOL	YUL BRYNNER	TARAS BULBA
ART DIRECTION:	EDWARD CARRERE	CHRISTINE KAUFMANN	NATALIA DUBROV
DIRECTOR OF PHOTOGRAPHY:	JOE MACDONALD	SAM WANAMAKER	FILIPENKO
EDITORS:	WILLIAM REYNOLDS, GENE MILFORD,	GUY ROLFE	PRINCE GRIGORY
	EDA WARREN AND FOLMAR BLANKSTED	BRAD DEXTER	SHILO
SOUND:	STAN COOLEY	PERRY LOPEZ	OSTAP BULBA
MUSIC:	FRANZ WAXMAN	GEORGE MACREADY	GOVERNOR
COSTUMES:	IZZY HERNE AND OLIVE KOENITZ	ILKA WINDISH	SOPHIA BULBA
		VLADIMIR IRMAN	GRISHA KUBENKO

Once a project of director Robert Aldrich for actor Burt Lancaster, 'Taras Bulba' emerged in the hands of action specialist J. Lee Thompson whose most noteworthy success had been 'The Guns of Navarone' (1961). The seven million dollar production was filmed at Salta in Argentina, an old Spanish colonial city in the foothills of the Andes. Ten thousand gauchos were hired to play the Cossack, Polish and Turkish armies; with a special elite of forty trained in the use of the sword by Curtis.

Curtis later remarked; "I liked working with Yul very much. That film's got some exquisite moments. God, I'll never forget that moment when the father shoots him; all you know of it is that little hole in the breastplate. I've never seen that on the screen before. Usually you see people smeared with blood yet all you saw was a tiny, clean little hole. Wow!"

It was during the making of this film that Curtis met his second wife Christine Kaufmann.

The 16th Century Ukraine. The Turkish and Polish armies are at war but when the Cossack warriors, led by Taras Bulba, join the fray Turkey is defeated. Bulba and his men are invited to a victory feast by the Polish leader Prince Grigory. However, at the celebration the Prince's forces attack the Cossacks. Bulba slashes off Grigory's right hand and heads for the Steppes. The Cossacks become a subjugated people but an uneasy peace develops and Bulba watches his sons Andrei and Ostap grow to maturity.

Andrei and Ostap are sent to the University of Kiev to learn the ways of the Poles. They face the hostility of the Polish students and University authorities but Andrei meets Natalia, the Governor's daughter and they fall in love. Natalia's brother and his gang attack the Bulba brothers but it is the former who is killed. Natalia's father sends her to the protection of the walled city of Dubno while the Bulbas return to the Steppes.

Taras receives word to amass ten thousand Cossacks at Dubno to fight in the Baltic wars. He uses this as a chance to repay Prince Grigory's former deceit and the Cossack hordes turn on the Polish army. The survivors flee to Dubno and Taras lays seige to the city. Starvation and Black Plague decimate the inhabitants of Dubno. Andrei slips into the city to bring food to Natalia but is captured and Natalia is condemned to be burned at the stake. Andrei bargains for her life and promises to lead the Polish soldiers on a raid to secure Cossack food. On leaving the city Andrei is shot dead by his father and the Cossacks are finally victorious over the Poles, capturing Dubno.

Harold Hecht-Avala Films

"Yul Brynner, who plays a great big brute of a Cossack chieftain, rides like a man Scotch taped into his saddle; Tony Curtis, who plays his son, has an accent that will pass as Russian when the Gowanus flows into the Don."

TIME

"But it is not what the characters say nor how they say it that commends this picture to the epic public so much as what they do while they are saying it. And what Tony Curtis does in particular would have left even Fairbanks Snr. breathless."

DAILY MAIL

FORTY POUNDS OF TROUBLE

U.S.A. 1962 – RUNNING TIME: 106 MINUTES
UNIVERSAL-INTERNATIONAL/CURTIS ENTERPRISES

		CAST	
DIRECTOR:	NORMAN JEWISON		
PRODUCER:	STAN MARGUILES		
SCREENPLAY:	MARION HARGROVE	TONY CURTIS	STEVE MCCLUSKEY
ART DIRECTION:	ALEXANDER GOLITZEN AND	SUZANNE PLESHETTE	CHRIS LOCKWOOD
	ROBERT CLATWORTHY	CLAIRE WILCOX	PENNY PIPER
DIRECTOR OF PHOTOGRAPHY:	JOE MACDONALD	LARRY STORCH	FLOYD
EDITOR:	MARJORIE FOWLER	HOWARD MORRIS	JULIUS
SOUND:	WALDON O. WATSON AND	EDWARD ANDREWS	HERMAN
	FRANK MCWHORTER	PHIL SILVERS	BERNIE FRIEDMAN
PRODUCTION MANAGER:	BOB LARSON	STUBBY KAYE	CRANSTON
MUSIC:	MORT LINDSEY	WARREN STEVENS	SWING
COSTUMES:	ROSEMARY ODELL/PETER SLADUTTI	MARY MURPHY	LIZ MCCLUSKEY
		KEVIN MCCARTHY	BLANCHARD

An unofficial remake of the Damon Runyon Depression classic 'Little Miss Marker', the amiable 'Forty Pounds of Trouble' surrounds Curtis with some top comic talent. Runyon's material has been well used by filmmakers; firstly under its original title in 1934 with Adolphe Menjou and Shirley Temple, then in 1949 as 'Sorrowful Jones' with Bob Hope, Lucille Ball and May Jane Saunders. Curtis himself would take a lesser role in the fourth version of the story eighteen years later.

Lake Tahoe, Nevada. Steve McCluskey runs the Villa D'Oro casino, owned by Bernie Friedman, and carries on a running feud with his ex-wife Liz over alimony payments. Liz retains a lawyer, Blanchard, and a team of private eyes, including Cranston, who are constantly vigilant as to his whereabouts. Should he enter California he will be arrested for non-payment of alimony.

At the casino Steve is left with six-year-old Penny Piper as a marker to cover her father's bet while he returns to San Francisco to raise the necessary money. Her father doesn't return and, to avoid bad publicity for the casino, Steve chooses to look after the child himself. Penny has only one wish; she wants to visit Disneyland in California. Friedman's niece Chris Lockwood visits the casino and is attracted to Steve when she sees how caring and thoughtful he is with Penny. Steve learns that Penny's father has been killed in a car crash leaving her an orphan. He decides to take her to Disneyland and devises an elaborate plan of disguises to ensure that he is not detected. Chris goes along so that it appears to be a visit by a married couple and their daughter.

However, Steve is caught and the story makes front page news along with the information about his harbouring a juvenile in a gambling house. Steve and Friedman face a court hearing. The judge is sympathetic and renews Friedman's gaming licence. When Steve and Chris agree to marry he also gives them permission to legally adopt Penny. The trio plan a honeymoon together at Disneyland.

"Tony Curtis is an actor who has learned his craft by doing it, and in 'Forty Pounds of Trouble' he shows that he has become a light comedian with few peers."

SUNDAY TELEGRAPH

"Tony has had better material but he has never made more of less. He skitters through his best scenes like a cat in pattens. He flicks a bad line away as a zillionaire might irritably flick a pearl out of an oyster. And when he does a slow burn you could fry an egg on his deadpan. Cary should approve."

TIME

The Kobal Collection

CAPTAIN NEWMAN M.D.

U.S.A. 1963 - RUNNING TIME: 126 MINUTES
BRENTWOOD/REYNARD FOR UNIVERSAL-INTERNATIONAL

DIRECTOR:	DAVID MILLER	CAST
PRODUCER:	ROBERT ARTHUR	
SCREENPLAY:	RICHARD L. BREEN AND	GREGORY PECK — CAPT. JOSIAH NEWMAN
PHOEBE AND HENRY EPHRON FROM THE NOVEL		TONY CURTIS — CORP. JACKSON LAIBOWITZ
	BY LEO ROSTEN	ANGIE DICKINSON — LT. FRANCIE CORUM
ART DIRECTION:	ALEXANDER GOLITZEN	EDDIE ALBERT — COL. NORVAL ALGATE BLISS
	AND ALFRED SWEENEY	BOBBY DARIN — CORP. JIM TOMPKINS
DIRECTOR OF PHOTOGRAPHY:	RUSSELL METTY	JAMES GREGORY — COL. EDGAR PYSER
EDITOR:	ALMA MACRORIE	JANE WITHERS — LT. GRACE BLODGETT
SOUND:	WALDON O. WATSON	BETHEL LESLIE — HELENE WINSTON
	AND BILL RUSSELL	ROBERT DUVALL — CAPT. PAUL CABOT WINSTON
PRODUCTION MANAGER:	JOSEPH BEHM	
COSTUMES:	ROSEMARY ODELL	

Despite the undisputed ability of many of those associated with 'Captain Newman M.D.' Tony Curtis's performance supplies the best reason for viewing the film. Based on a bestselling novel the film has other points of interest; as a convincing display of Bobby Darin's acting prowess, as an early appearance by future Oscar-winner Robert Duvall and as Gregory Peck's first film after his Oscar-winning 'To Kill a Mocking-Bird' (1962). Curtis so capably handles his carefully tailored role of a resourceful ward orderly that he puts Peck's dullness and the plot's uneasy mix of comedy and drama well into the shade.

1944. Captain Josiah Newman is in charge of the neuro-psychiatric department at Camp Colfax, an Army Air Base. He must constantly combat the prejudiced attitudes of his superiors to provide proper care for the many cases that he encounters. Newman's commanding officer Colonel Pyser is annoyed that Newman grounds so many men and that his ward has the slowest return-to-duty rate in his entire command. Newman is sustained in his work by lovely nurse Francie Corum. He also learns from the ward orderly, Corporal Jackson Laibowitz, who is completely untrained in psychiatric care but has an intuitive understanding of peoples' problems. Newman allows Laibowitz special privileges and the wheeler-dealer corporal becomes an indispensable figure in the ward.

Among the men whom Newman and Laibowitz attempt to help is Colonel Bliss, a man whose mind has cracked under the strain of all the men he has sent into combat and who have never returned. He runs amok armed with a knife but Laibowitz is able to restrain him. Later Bliss ascends a water-tank tower and jumps to his death. Corporal Tompkins has been decorated for bravery in thirty-four missions but believes himself to be a coward for failing to rescue a friend from a burning plane. Newman helps him to recover his self-esteem and he returns to duty, dying in combat. Captain Winston enters the ward in a catatonic state but Newman slowly draws him out and he too begins to recover. Although Newman is plagued with doubts as to the value of his work when he is only returning men to the hazards of combat, he knows that he must continue.

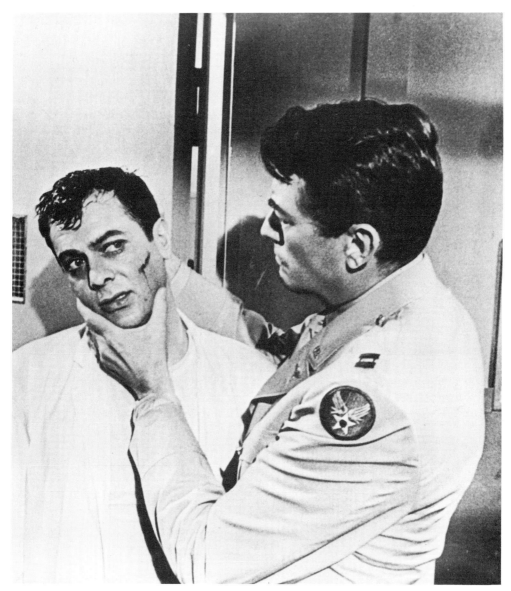

Gregory Peck   Brentwood-Reynard Productions

"If there had not been Tony Curtis as a ward orderly I might have needed one of those paper bags they provide on aircraft. Curtis, as the fast-talking Corporal Laibowitz - is the very, very good bit of the film."

DAILY HERALD

"Tony Curtis, in a performance exactly opposite to Peck's is a knockout. A conniving, fast-talking extrovert, Curtis gives a superlative comedy portrayal, a character role of the sort he too seldom takes but plays superbly."

HOLLYWOOD REPORTER

"Curtis has some good moments but essentially he is the pivotal figure in the film's secondary comic shenanigans, the portions that, being somewhat contrived and excessively sentimental, subtract from the potential of the whole."

VARIETY

WILD AND WONDERFUL

U.S.A. 1964 – RUNNING TIME: 88 MINUTES
UNIVERSAL-INTERNATIONAL

		CAST	
DIRECTOR:	MICHAEL ANDERSON		
PRODUCER:	HAROLD HECHT		
SCREENPLAY:	LARRY MARKES, MICHAEL MORRIS	TONY CURTIS	TERRY WILLIAMS
	AND WALDO SALT FROM A STORY BY	CHRISTINE KAUFMANN	GISELLE PONCHON
	RICHARD M. POWELL, PHILLIP RAPP AND	LARRY STORCH	RUFUS GIBBS
	DOROTHY CRIDER	PIERRE OLAF	JACQUOT
ART DIRECTION:	ALEXANDER GOLITZEN	MARTY INGELS	DOC BAILEY
	AND EDWARD HAWORTH	JACQUES AUBUCHON	PAPA PONCHON
DIRECTOR OF PHOTOGRAPHY:	JOSEPH LA SHELLE	SARAH MARSHALL	PAMELA
EDITOR:	GENE MILFORD	MARCEL DALIO	DR REYNARD
SOUND:	WALDON O. WATSON AND	JULES MUNSHIN	ROUSSELEAU
	JOE LAPIS	MARCEL HILLAIRE	INSP. DUVIVIER
PRODUCTION MANAGER:	BOB LARSON		
MUSIC:	MORTON STEVENS		
COSTUMES:	VALENTINO-ROME/		
	ROSEMARY ODELL		

Known throughout its production as 'Monsieur Cognac' this glamorous Curtis comedy allowed him to work with his then wife Christine Kaufmann. Paris was recreated on the sound stages at Universal in downtown Hollywood. Art directors Alexander Golitzen and Edward Haworth produced a detailed replica of the Montmartre area and the gowns worn by Miss Kaufmann were especially created by Valentino of Rome.

Monsieur Cognac, a pampered French poodle, is one of the best known film stars in Paris. He lives in an elaborate mansion with his owner Papa Ponchon and his daughter, film star Giselle. Cognac is devoted to Giselle but has a weakness for drink and a secret love for Pink Poupee, a female French poodle who is part of 'Pamela's Performing Poodles'. One evening Cognac sneaks out of the mansion and makes for Poupee's nightclub. He arrives too late to see Poupee but is befriended by flautist Terry Williams and together they get drunk.

When Cognac is discovered missing Papa calls the police but Terry proves his innocence and when he meets Giselle it is love at first sight. The course of their love does not run smoothly as they must contend with Papa's disapproval and Cognac's jealousy. They decide to elope but attempt to placate Papa by agreeing to spend their wedding night at his house. Cognac refuses to leave their bedroom and when Terry attempts to drug the dog Cognac switches glasses and Terry is knocked out cold. When he awakens he has a stormy argument with Giselle who refuses to leave Cognac so that they may spend their honeymoon alone. Subsequently Terry leaves Giselle.

Terry formulates a plan to win back Giselle and get rid of Cognac. When the dog is being honoured with a television special Terry arrives at the house with two of his colleagues from the 'Terry Williams Trio' and Pink Poupee. Complete pandemonium breaks out but Giselle and Papa are resigned to the fact that Cognac needs female company. Now that Cognac is otherwise engaged Terry and Giselle set off for Rome and their long-delayed honeymoon.

"Curtis breezes through his role amiably and professionally and Miss Kaufmann is a most decorative romantic partner."

VARIETY

Larry Storch (right)   Universal-International

"Tony Curtis sparkles as the man who believes his wife, not her dog, is man's best friend. He sparks the picture with his attack, timing and characterization. Miss Kaufmann, a delicate and pretty girl, is somewhat ethereal for this sort of fast farce. She is appealing but this kind of role does not appear to be her forte."

HOLLYWOOD REPORTER

GOODBYE CHARLIE

U.S.A. 1964 – RUNNING TIME: 116 MINUTES
TWENTIETH CENTURY FOX-VENICE PRODUCTION

		CAST	
DIRECTOR:	VINCENTE MINNELLI		
PRODUCER:	DAVID WEISBART		
SCREENPLAY:	HARRY KURNITZ FROM THE	TONY CURTIS	GEORGE TRACY
	PLAY BY GEORGE AXELROD	DEBBIE REYNOLDS	CHARLIE SOREL (FEMALE)
ART DIRECTION:	JACK MARTIN SMITH	PAT BOONE	BRUCE MINTON
	AND RICHARD DAY	JOANNA BARNES	JANIE
DIRECTOR OF PHOTOGRAPHY:	MILTON KRASNER	LAURA DEVON	RUSTY
EDITOR:	JOHN W. HOLMES	WALTER MATTHAU	SIR LEOPOLD SARTORI
SOUND:	W.D.FLICK AND	ELLEN MCRAE	FRANNY
	ELMER RAGUSE	MARTIN GABEL	MORTON CRAFT
MUSIC:	ANDRE PREVIN	ROGER CARMEL	INSPECTOR
COSTUMES:	HELEN ROSE	HARRY MADDEN	CHARLIE (MALE)

George Axelrod was previously responsible for 'The Seven Year Itch' and 'Will Success Spoil Rock Hunter?'. His tasteless, involved farce 'Goodbye Charlie' had been a Broadway success in 1960 for Lauren Bacall and the first choice for the film version had been Marilyn Monroe.

The film's acting honours belong to Curtis's former colleague from the Dramatic Workshop in The 1940s, Walter Matthau. Matthau's Alexander Korda-like figure steals the show whenever he appears. 'Goodbye Charlie' scraped into the list of top box-office successes of 1965 at the twentieth position having taken three million, four hundred thousand dollars.

Aboard the yacht Aphrodite a party is in progress hosted by Sir Leopold Sartori. Sartori's wife Rusty is dancing with infamous womaniser Charlie Sorel. When the couple slip below decks Sir Leopold follows them with a gun and shoots Charlie as he attempts to escape through a porthole.

Charlie's best friend George Tracy is named executor of the will and arrives to oversee the funeral. George's first night at Charlie's home is interrupted by passing playboy Bruce Minton who has picked up a soaking wet blonde on the highway. When Bruce leaves, the girl tells George that she is Charlie somehow reincarnated as a woman. George is incredulous but is convinced when she recounts the details of some previous escapades that only the real Charlie would know. Passing as Charlie's widow she calls herself Mrs Sorel and exploits her newfound womanhood by flirting with Bruce and blackmailing the society wives that Charlie had seduced. George is horrified by her behaviour but attracted to her at the same time.

Sir Leopold also takes a shine to Mrs Sorel and attempts to seduce her one evening. George returns home to find her fighting off Sir Leopold's advances. When Rusty arrives she shoots Mrs Sorel who tumbles into the sea. Moments later Charlie reappears in the form of a dog accompanied by a pretty owner who bears a striking resemblance to the just departed Mrs Sorel. George and the woman strike up a friendship whilst Charlie laps up some vodka.

"Curtis lends the proper anxious note to the whole proceedings. He and Reynolds make their work count as much as script will permit under Vincent Minnelli's direction."
HOLLYWOOD REPORTER

"Miss Reynolds tackles the role manfully in 'Goodbye Charlie'. And Tony Curtis, as the dead man's best friend, flaps around, game to the end."
DAILY WORKER

Twentieth Century-Fox/Venice Productions

SEX AND THE SINGLE GIRL

U.S.A. 1964 - RUNNING TIME: 114 MINUTES
RICHARD QUINE-REYNARD PRODUCTION

		CAST	
DIRECTOR:	RICHARD QUINE		
PRODUCER:	WILLIAM T. ORR		
SCREENPLAY:	JOSEPH HELLER, DAVID R. SHWARTZ	TONY CURTIS	BOB WESTON
	FROM THE BOOK BY HELEN GURLEY BROWN	NATALIE WOOD	HELEN BROWN
ART DIRECTION:	GARY O'DELL	HENRY FONDA	FRANK
DIRECTOR OF PHOTOGRAPHY:	CHARLES LANG JR.	LAUREN BACALL	SYLVIA
EDITOR:	DAVID WAGES	MEL FERRER	RUDY
SOUND:	M.A. MERRICK	FRAN JEFFRIES	GRETCHEN
MUSIC:	NEAL HEFTI	LESLIE PARRISH	SUSAN
COSTUMES:	EDITH HEAD	EDWARD EVERETT HORTON	CHIEF
		OTTO KRUGER	DR ANDERSON
		HOWARD ST. JOHN	GEORGE RANDALL
		LARRY STORCH	MOTORCYCLE COP
		STUBBY KAYE	CABBY

Helen Brown's book had achieved sales of over three million copies in paperback and Warner Brothers paid an estimated two hundred thousand dollars for the right to make a film which bears absolutely no relation to the book. Among those responsible for the screenplay was one Joseph Heller, author of Catch 22. In her autobiography, 'By Myself', Lauren Bacall wrote; "I returned to California mid-November for another film, 'Sex and the Single Girl': a very good cast — Natalie Wood, Hank Fonda, Tony Curtis — but not a very good film." In America during 1965 it was the number fifteen attraction at the box-office with four million dollars to its credit.

In South Africa the local censor decided to delete the first two words from the title thus it was shown as 'The Single Girl'.

Bob Weston is the successful editor of 'Stop' magazine, an unscrupulous scandal sheet, the latest issue of which slanders famous sexologist Helen Brown claiming she is a 23-year-old virgin. West aims to check the veracity of that statement personally before the next issue.

Bob decides to masquerade as his neighbour Frank and visit Dr. Brown's clinic. Frank manufactures ladies' hosiery and his obsession with work leads to constant rows with his lovely wife Sylvia. Bob uses Frank's problems as his own and consults Helen who is flattered by his attentions. Helen's colleague, psychiatrist Rudi, is also attracted to her when he reads she may be a virgin.

Bob's own romance with singer Gretchen is under some strain but he is now genuinely attracted to Helen who is beginning to lose interest in his case. Meanwhile Frank has been following Helen's advice, relayed through Bob, and has never been happier. Helen tells Bob that she will only see him again if she can meet Sylvia. Bob asks Gretchen to pretend to be Sylvia but she refuses and his secretary goes along to the appointment with Helen. Gretchen relents and also turns up along with the real Sylvia who promptly has Frank arrested for bigamy. At 'Stop' Bob refuses to write his exclusive story on Helen and is fired.

When Helen visits Sylvia she sees a picture of Frank and the plot is unravelled allowing Frank to be released from jail. Eventually Frank and Sylvia are reunited, Bob and Helen patch up their differences and Gretchen and Rudi find solace in each other's company.

Natalie Wood

Richard Quine-Reynard Productions

"Curtis registers exceptionally well when detailing supposed marital problems to adviser. His timing in confessing to "inadequacies" shows great comic talent."

VARIETY

"Curtis is quick and facile as the magazine writer."

HOLLYWOOD REPORTER

THE GREAT RACE

U.S.A. 1965 – RUNNING TIME: 163 MINUTES
A PATRICIA-JALEM-REYNARD PRODUCTION

DIRECTOR:	BLAKE EDWARDS	CAST	
PRODUCER:	MARTIN JUROW		
ASSOCIATE PRODUCER:	DICK CROCKETT	JACK LEMMON	PROFESSOR FATE
SCREENPLAY:	BLAKE EDWARDS AND ARTHUR ROSS	TONY CURTIS	THE GREAT LESLIE
PRODUCTION DESIGNER:	FERNANDO CARRERE	NATALIE WOOD	MAGGIE DUBOIS
DIRECTOR OF PHOTOGRAPHY:	RUSSELL HARLAN	PETER FALK	MAX
EDITOR:	RALPH E. WINTERS	KEENAN WYNN	HEZEKIAH
SOUND:	M.A.MERRICK	DOROTHY PROVINE	LILY OLAY
MUSIC:	HENRY MANCINI	ARTHUR O'CONNELL	HENRY GOODBODY
COSTUMES:	DONFELD	VIVIAN VANCE	HESTER GOODBODY
		ROSS MARTIN	ROLFE VON STUPPE
		LARRY STORCH	TEXAS JACK

Dedicated to 'Mr. Laurel and Mr. Hardy', 'The Great Race' is a gargantuan comedy which works on the principle that if you include every gag and comic device known to film-makers then some of it is bound to be funny. And some of it is. A twelve million dollar production which filmed on locations in Salzburg, Vienna and Paris 'The Great Race' belongs to the era of elephantine film comedies that numbered 'Those Magnificent Men in their Flying Machines' (1965) and 'It's A Mad, Mad, Mad, Mad World' (1963) among its ranks.

The film was awarded the Silver Prize as 'Best Comedy' at the 1965 Moscow Film Festival and won one American Academy Award for best sound effects.

New York, 1908. A deadly rivalry exists between the Great Leslie and the dastardly Professor Fate. When Leslie enters his gleaming white 'Leslie Special' in the first New York to Paris road race Fate constructs his own vehicle, the malevolently black 'Hannibal 8', and enters the race with his faithful sidekick Max. Fate's booby-traps sabotage most of the other competitors before they can even start but the race is on and also in the running is the indomitable journalist Maggie Dubois who has cajoled her boss into allowing her to drive in, and report on, the race.

Out in the West Maggie is forced to abandon her 'Stanley Steamer' vehicle but the gallant Leslie rides to her rescue. Under cover of a mammoth saloon brawl Fate destroys the petrol supply in a remote town leaving Leslie stranded. Maggie has access to petrol but she insists that Leslie must take her along for the entire race. The two rivals are bumper to bumper again in Alaska as they realise they are drifting towards the Siberian coast on a slowly melting iceberg. Both cars reach the Balkan state of Carpania but not before Fate has kidnapped Maggie.

Carpania is ruled by the foppish Prince Hapnick and when Baron von Stuppe notices the striking resemblance between Fate and Hapnick he decides to overthrow the ruler replacing the Prince with the Professor. Leslie manages to rescue the strong-willed Maggie during a sprawling pie-fight and eventually both rivals are back en route for Paris. However, nearing the finishing line Leslie stops long enough to kiss Maggie and thus allows Fate to claim victory. Fate is enraged that Leslie has allowed him to win. The only solution is a rematch — in the opposite direction.

Natalie Wood   Particia-Jalem-Reynard Productions

"He gives his hero's role a touch of the dense, but what helps the laughs immeasurably is his insistence on reality. He is the stand-in for the audience as the insanity mounts."

HOLLYWOOD REPORTER

"Tony Curtis, dazzling white from head to foot, has mainly to keep springing to the rescue as the knight of the motor car."

MONTHLY FILM BULLETIN

BOEING-BOEING

U.S.A. 1965 – RUNNING TIME: 102 MINUTES
PARAMOUNT PRODUCTION

DIRECTOR:	JOHN RICH	CAST	
PRODUCER:	HAL B. WALLIS		
ASSOCIATE PRODUCER:	PAUL NATHAN	TONY CURTIS:	BERNARD LAWRENCE
SCREENPLAY:	EDWARD ANHALT FROM THE PLAY	JERRY LEWIS	ROBERT REED
	BY MARC CAMOLETTI	DANY SAVAL	JACQUELINE GRIEUX
ART DIRECTION:	HAL PEREIRA	CHRISTIANE SCHMIDTMER	LISE BRUNER
	AND WALTER TYLER	SUZANNA LEIGH	VICKY HAWKINS
DIRECTOR OF PHOTOGRAPHY:	LUCIEN BALLARD	THELMA RITTER	BERTHA
EDITORS:	WARREN LOW AND	LOMAX STUDY	PIERRE
	ARCHIE MARSHEK		
SOUND:	HAROLD LEWIS		
MUSIC:	NEAL HEFTI		
COSTUMES:	EDITH HEAD		

On paper the comedy team of Curtis and his friend of many years, Jerry Lewis, seems an unlikely one. However, they work surprisingly well in this amusing adaptation of a long-running, frenetically paced stage hit. Lewis, normally the master of madcap lunacy, is remarkably subdued and performs effectively within (for him) a conventional setting. Until his brilliant performance in 'King of Comedy' (1982) this was his only straight role.

Paris. Journalist Bernard Lawrence believes that he has the perfect arrangement. Helped by his overworked housekeeper Bertha he is engaged to three girls at once, all air hostesses who never meet because of conflicting schedules. Vicky is with British United, Lise works for Lufthansa and Jacqueline is with Air France. Bernard runs to a meticulously-planned routine and Bertha ensures that each girl receives her favourite food, clothes etc.

One day all his plans come adrift. His old friend Robert Reed arrives and announces that he is moving in, whilst the airlines announce faster planes and new schedules. Robert becomes suspicious when both Vicky and Lise introduce themselves as Bernard's bride to be. Life is becoming increasingly hectic for Bernard and Bertha when all three girls arrive at his apartment at the same time. Bernard takes Jacqueline to dinner, Robert is forced to entertain Vicky and Lisa is left asleep in the apartment. Vicky finds that she is instantly attracted to Robert and insists that they rush to tell Bernard. They arrive at the apartment at the same time as Bernard and Jacqueline; Bertha is on the point of leaving and Lise is just waking up. Finally the three girls are face to face but Bernard's courage deserts him and he flees the apartment, closely followed by Robert. The two men hail a taxi driven by a very pretty young girl. She explains that she is one of only three female taxi drivers in Paris. They share an apartment but never see each other because of the shifts they work. Bernard and Robert look at each other with a familiar glint in their eyes.

"It doesn't set out to do very much more than transfer the highly successful farce to the screen, but – with the exception of the three girls, each more incompetent that the next – it succeeds. Which is more a tribute to Tony Curtis, Jerry Lewis and Thelma Ritter than anyone else. They have the proper feeling for the mechanical aspects of farce, and they go through the opening and shutting of doors with the ease of true professionals."

GUARDIAN

Jerry Lewis

Paramount Productions

"Tony Curtis and Jerry Lewis, apparently gods of dissimilar races, prove to be brothers under the skin, and make an astonishingly effective comedy team."

TIMES

NOT WITH MY WIFE YOU DON'T

U.S.A. 1966 – RUNNING TIME: 118 MINUTES
FERNWOOD-REYNARD PRODUCTION

DIRECTOR:	NORMAN PANAMA	**CAST**	
PRODUCER:	NORMAN PANAMA		
ASSOCIATE PRODUCER:	JOEL FREEMAN	**TONY CURTIS**	TOM FERRIS
SCREENPLAY:	NORMAN PANAMA, LARRY GELBART	**VIRNA LISI**	JULIE FERRIS
	AND PETER BARNES	**GEORGE C. SCOTT**	'TANK' MARTIN
ART DIRECTION:	EDWARD CARRERE	**CARROLL O'CONNOR**	GENERAL PARKER
DIRECTOR OF PHOTOGRAPHY:	CHARLES LANG	**RICHARD EASTHAM**	GENERAL WALTERS
	AND PAUL BEESON	**EDDIE RYDER**	SGT. GILROY
EDITOR:	AARON STELL	**GEORGE TYNE**	SGT. DOGERTY
SOUND:	STANLEY JONES	**ANN DORAN**	DORIS PARKER
MUSIC:	JOHNNY WILLIAMS	**DONNA DANTON**	NURSE SALLY ANN
COSTUMES:	EDITH HEAD	**NATALIE CORE**	LILLIAN WALTERS
		BOBE HOPE	HIMSELF

Director Norman Panama had once formed a successful partnership with fellow comedy specialist Melvin Frank. In the 1930s they began writing material for Bob Hope's radio shows and carried over their collaboration into the cinema writing scripts for 'My Favourite Blonde' (1942) and the Hope-Crosby-Lamour 'Road' films. After jointly directing several films, including Danny Kaye's 'The Court Jester' (1956) they went their separate ways with Frank enjoying the lion's share of any solo success. 'Not With My Wife You Don't' is probably the best of a lacklustre group of films directed by Panama, aided by Curtis's comic vitality and George C. Scott who is engagingly larger than life in a rare light role. As a favour to Panama, Bob Hope appears as himself entertaining the troops at a service show.

London. Tom Ferris is the perfect military attache but his wife, Julie, is less than enamoured by his obsessive devotion to duty. One day at the American Embassy Tom catches sight of his old buddy 'Tank' Martin and recalls an eventful period fourteen years earlier.

In 1952, during the Korean conflict, Tom and 'Tank' were colleagues in the air and rivals on the ground. After one brawl Tom winds up in hospital where he meets beautiful nurse Julie. When 'Tank' finally sees Julie he sets out to wine and dine her, ordering Tom to spend one month's convalescence in Tokyo. By the time Tom returns Julie cannot choose between her two suitors. On his next mission 'Tank' crashes but is rescued and spends a month in Manila. Once Tom knows his friend is safe he lies to Julie that 'Tank' is dead and the two marry. It is only later that the couple learn of 'Tank's' miraculous survival.

Back in the present Tom flies to Copenhagen and 'Tank' plans a reunion with Julie. When 'Tank' belatedly discovers that Tom destroyed evidence that told of his survival in 1952 he has him sent on an Arctic Survival Course to Labrador and begins charming Julie all over again. When Tom makes contact from Labrador he can only talk about army business which angers Julie who demands a divorce. Tom disguises himself as an Arab sheik, steals a jet and flies to London. There 'Tank' tells him that he must pay more attention to Julie and the couple are reconciled. Three years later Tom and 'Tank' are happily working together while Tom and Julie are contentedly married with two children.

"Tony Curtis is enviably confident as the sweet-talking, smooth-operating Tom and has rarely been better."

SUNDAY EXPRESS

Fernwood-Reynard Productions

"Though the film has its downs there are corresponding ups, mainly when Mr Curtis is centre screen. His comic persona of the wheeler-dealer who sometimes gets caught in his own cleverness is given several excellent opportunities..."

TIMES

DROP DEAD DARLING

USA: ARRIVIDERCI BABY

UNITED KINGDOM 1966 – RUNNING TIME: 100 MINUTES
SEVEN ARTS

		CAST	
DIRECTOR:	KEN HUGHES		
PRODUCER:	KEN HUGHES		
ASSOCIATE PRODUCERS:	RICHARD MCWHORTER	TONY CURTIS	NICK
	GREG MORRISON	ROSANNA SCHIAFFINO	FRANCESCA
SCREENPLAY:	KEN HUGHES FROM THE STORY	LIONEL JEFFRIES	PARKER
	'THE CAREFUL MAN'	NANCY KWAN	BABY
	BY RICHARD DEEMING	ZSA ZSA GABOR	GIGI
ART DIRECTION:	SEAMUS FLANNERY	FENELLA FIELDING	LADY FENELLA FAWCETT
DIRECTOR OF PHOTOGRAPHY:	DENYS COOP	ANNA QUAYLE	AUNT MIRIAM
EDITOR:	JOHN SHIRLEY	WARREN MITCHELL	COUNT DE RIENZI
SOUND:	JOHN MITCHELL	MISCHA AUER	RICH ITALIAN
PRODUCTION MANAGER:	JAMES WARE	NOEL PURCELL	DANIEL O'FLANNERY
MUSIC:	DENNIS FARNON		
COSTUMES:	ELIZABETH HAFFENDEN		
	AND JOAN BRIDGE		

A variation on 'Kind Hearts and Coronets', with Curtis as a contemporary Bluebeard, 'Drop Dead Darling' brought Curtis to Europe for his first British film. Locations used by director Ken Hughes included Monte Carlo, Ile du Levant, Cote d'Azur and parts of England. Shepperton Studios were the company's base for the interior sequences. The film was not a success.

Con man Nick Johnson has hit on a winning formula. He marries rich women and devises ingenious means of disposing of them. As a youth he had perfected this technique when, adopted by Aunt Miriam, he dispatched her with a few technical adjustments to her harp, resulting in an electronic explosion.

Wife number one for Nick is the oft-wed international beauty Gigi who meets her maker in the cockpit of a heavenwardbound space missile that she was supposed to launch. Wife number two is Lady Fenella Fawcett, a hale and hearty English lady to the manor born. Nick arranges an accident for Fenella. She goes horse riding and jumps a fence with a lengthy descent on the other side. Nick's servant Parker suggests that beautiful Francesca, widow of a wealthy Italian Count, as a suitable candidate to become Mrs Johnson the Third.

Unknown to Nick the Count's considerable fortune has passed to his brother Maximillian and not Francesca. Once married he realises that he has met his equal — Francesca appears to be planning his demise in much the same manner as he is planning hers. During their plotting and counter-plotting Nick and Francesca fall genuinely in love. Eventually they abandon their murderous schemes to settle down and live happily ever after. The are finally pictured in humble accommodation, with spaghetti bubbling on the stove, and children running all over the house.

"He performs with jaunting and mannered style, Hughes' direction allowing him to acknowledge the presence of the audience with knowing takes and devilish asides. Few actors could so successfully get away with the improbable flashback sequence in which he plays himself as a leering lad at an orphanage."

HOLLYWOOD REPORTER

Seven Arts

DON'T MAKE WAVES

U.S.A. 1967 – RUNNING TIME: 97 MINUTES
FILMWAYS-REYNARD

DIRECTOR:	ALEXANDER MACKENDRICK	
PRODUCERS:	JOHN CALLEY AND	
	MARTIN RANSOHOFF	
ASSOCIATE PRODUCER:	JULIAN BERCOVICI	
SCREENPLAY:	IRA WALLACH AND GEORGE KIRGO	
	FROM THE NOVEL 'MUSCLE BEACH'	
	BY WALLACH	
ART DIRECTION:	GEORGE W. DAVIS	
	AND EDWARD CARFAGNO	
DIRECTOR OF PHOTOGRAPHY:	PHILIP LATHROP	
EDITORS:	RITA ROLAND AND THOMAS STANFORD	
PRODUCTION MANAGER:	EDWARD WOEHLER	
MUSIC:	VIC MIZZY	
COSTUMES:	DONFELD	

CAST

TONY CURTIS	CARLO COFIELD
CLAUDIA CARDINALE	LAURA CALIFATTI
ROBERT WEBBER	ROD PRESCOTT
JOANNA BARNES	DIANA PRESCOTT
SHARON TATE	MALIBU
DAVID DRAPER	HARRY HOLLARD
MORT SAHL	SAM LINGONBERRY
DUB TAYLOR	ELECTRICIAN
ANN ELDER	MILLIE GUNDER
CHESTER YORTON	TED GUNDER

A reunion with Alexander Mackendrick, the director of 'Sweet Smell of Success', brought a mixed response from both critics and the public. Mackendrick had directed 'Whisky Galore' (1948), 'The Man in the White Suit' (1951) and 'The Ladykillers' (1955) for Ealing Studios. Yet despite his assured comic touch the elements here just refuse to gel into a satisfactory whole. He has not directed for the cinema since this film, having accepted a post as Dean of the Film Department of the Institute of Arts in California.

Some of the technical details of the comedy stunts in 'Don't Make Waves' are interesting — the parachute jump necessitated thirty-five jumps to capture it for the camera, and when the house is swept over a cliff it is a mixture of three houses; one on a soundstage that could tip to an eighteen degree angle, a second upside-down house on a soundstage and a third at the foot of a Santa Monica cliff on the debris of a real house which had been destroyed by a mudslide.

Professor Carlo Cofield is fired from his college position after being caught in a police raid on a student party. On the Pacific coast road he meets Laura who accidentally destroys his Volkswagen, containing his money and possessions, and then proceeds to set fire to his trousers. He is left with nothing in the world. Laura offers him a bed for the night but when her lover, Prescott Brandon, arrives Carlo is forced to spend the night on the beach.

Next morning Carlo goes for a swim and is knocked unconscious by surfboarder Malibu to whom he is instantly attracted. Carlo rifles through Prescott's belongings, discovering that he is a married man and later fast talks his way into a job as a swimming pool salesman. He learns that Malibu lives in an old bus with muscleman Harry but that Harry is worried that sex is ruining his physique. Harry is also a devoted reader of the astrology column by Mme. Lavinia. Carlo winds up buying a house perched on a seaside cliff from Sadakichi, a Japanese businessman about to start Sunrise Estates. Carlo hopes to sell him a pool for every house.

Carlo learns that Malibu can sky-dive and plans a big publicity stunt. Prescott rejects the idea so Carlo goes into business for himself, guaranteeing to install the Sunrise Estate pools within a fortnight. During the skydiving stunt Carlo is inadvertently ejected from the plane but is saved by Malibu. With help from Mme. Valentine Carlo convinces Harry that sex is bad for him and Malibu moves in with Carlo. Malibu is addicted to television and Carlo finds her boring. He tries to get rid of her by turning muscleman and claiming that their relationship must remain platonic.

Claudia Cardinale   Filmways-Reynard

It rains for days and Carlo's business deal is in jeopardy. However, after many complications (including Carlo's house being swept down the side of the cliff) all is resolved. Harry and Malibu are reunited, Prescott returns to his wife and takes over the swimming pool deal and Carlo and Laura drive off in search of the simple life.

"Stars, Tony Curtis and Claudia Cardinale, director Alexander Mackendrick: three talents wasted."

SUNDAY TIMES

"Don't Make Waves is one of the most underrated comedies of the season. Alexander Mackendrick's direction is longer on quiet chuckles than noisy belly laughs and Tony Curtis gives his most perceptive performance since 'Sweet Smell of Success' also directed by Mackendrick."

VILLAGE VOICE

"The one gem out of nine million bad Tony Curtis comedy vehicles."   **TV MOVIES**

THE CHASTITY BELT

(USA: ON MY WAY TO THE CRUSADES I MET A GIRL WHO...)

ITALY 1967 – RUNNING TIME: 110 MINUTES
JULIA FILM PRODUCTION

DIRECTOR:	PASQUALE FESTA CAMPANILE	**CAST**	
PRODUCER:	FRANCESCO MAZZEI		
SCREENPLAY:	LUIGI MAGNI	**TONY CURTIS**	GUERRANDO DA MONTONE
	AND LARRY GELBART	**MONICA VITTI**	BOCCADORO
ART DIRECTION:	PIERO POLETTO	**HUGH GRIFFITH**	SULTAN OF BARI
DIRECTOR OF PHOTOGRAPHY:	CARLO DI PALMA	**JOHN RICHARDSON**	DROGONE
EDITOR:	CHARLES NELSON	**IVO GARRANI**	DUKE OF PANDOLFO
SOUND:	AURELIO VERONA	**NINO CASTELNUOVO**	MARCULFO
PRODUCTION COORDINATOR:	LUCIANO PIPERNO	**FRANCO SPORTELLI**	BERTUCCIO
MUSIC:	RIZ ORTOLANI	**LAURO GAZZOLO**	HERMIT
COSTUMES:	DANILO DONATI		

Curtis's first Italian film was made during the rough winter weather of 1966-7 when, unusually, Curtis found that he did not get on well with his leading lady Monica Vitti here playing a character called Golden Lips. The bawdy comedy ran into trouble over its length and its title. A mildly saucy farce, the film received an X certificate in Britain and was cut from an original running time of one hour forty minutes to just seventy three — a virtually unprecedented deletion of over half an hour. The Italian title is 'La Cintura de Castita' which was literally translated as 'The Chastity Belt' although in some areas it was known as 'A Funny Thing Happened on the Way to the Crusades'.

The 11th Century. Guerrando da Montone is knighted by the Duke of Pandolfo for his valour and is entitled to the ownership of as much land as he can travel over by horse before sundown. That evening he arrives exhausted at the house of gamekeeper Bertuccio and is instantly attracted to his daughter, the fiery Boccadoro. The two meet again during a stag hunt but Boccadoro resents Guerrando's chauvinistic attitude and their courtship does not run smoothly. At a banquet Guerrando offers marriage but Boccadoro refuses. He then threatens to behead her father and she agrees to a wedding because, at heart, she does love Guerrando. Before the marriage can be consummated Guerrando is ordered to take arms with the Duke of Pandolfo and lay siege against the Sultan of Bari. He reluctantly leaves his bride and locks her in a chastity belt to ensure that she remains faithful during his absence.

Boccadoro dresses in golden armour and rides after Guerrando. She is challenged by Drogone and defeats him in combat. While Guerrando sleeps Drogone steals the key to the chastity belt and replaces it with a fake. Boccadoro wants Guerrando to free her and she goes to him but they are both captured and taken to the castle of the lecherous Sultan. The Sultan takes Guerrando's key and chases Boccadoro around the battlements. Guerrando however, has switched keys and, managing to escape, rescues Boccadoro when Emperor Ludwig II marches on the castle. Boccadoro and Guerrando ride off to a nearby beach but their key does not unlock the belt. Later Drogone (who was Ludwig in disguise) rides by and gives them the genuine key, thus allowing the couple to consummate their marriage.

"The film is surprisingly inventive and sustains comic earthiness at a fairly brisk gallop... Tony Curtis and Monica Vitti are not at their best but the latter is much more at home in her role."
VARIETY

Monica Vitti

THE BOSTON STRANGLER

U.S.A. 1968 – RUNNING TIME: 116 MINUTES
TWENTIETH CENTURY-FOX

DIRECTOR:	RICHARD FLEISCHER	**CAST**
PRODUCER:	ROBERT FRYER	
ASSOCIATE PRODUCER:	JAMES CRESSON	
SCREENPLAY:	EDWARD ANHALT FROM THE BOOK	
	BY GEROLD FRANK	
ART DIRECTION:	JACK MARTIN SMITH	
	AND RICHARD DAY	
DIRECTOR OF PHOTOGRAPHY:	RICHARD KLINE	
EDITOR:	MARION ROTHMAN	
SOUND:	DON BASSMAN AND	
	DAVID DOCKENDORF	
PRODUCTION MANAGER:	ERIC STACEY	
MUSIC:	LIONEL NEWMAN	

CAST	
TONY CURTIS	ALBERT DE SALVO
HENRY FONDA	JOHN S. BOTTOMLY
GEORGE KENNEDY	PHIL DI NATALE
MIKE KELLIN	JULIAN SOSHNICK
HURD HATFIELD	TERENCE HUNTLEY
MURRAY HAMILTON	FRANK MCAFEE
JEFF COREY	JOHN ASGIERSSON
SALLY KELLERMAN	DIANNE CLUNY
WILLIAM MARSHALL	EDWARD W. BROOKE

Having largely concentrated on light comedy throughout the 1960s Curtis found that his career had lost its momentum; especially given the dismal failure of recent ventures like 'The Chastity Belt'. He needed to revitalise his career, he needed a challenge which would once again assert his maturity as an actor, and 'The Boston Strangler' fitted the bill admirably. In Hollywood, where memories can be very short, there was much resistance to the idea of Curtis playing The Strangler. There had been a seven month search for an actor to portray De Salvo and Curtis only won the part when he used his own initiative. Using his own make-up he made his features unrecognisable, took some snapshots and submitted them to Twentieth Century-Fox. One executive felt that whoever it was seemed right for the part, and only then was it revealed that Curtis was the name behind the face. He was cast and production began in January 1968.

The film simplifies both De Salvo's motivation and his home life but Curtis's anguished Jekyll and Hyde murderer is his finest hour as a dramatic performer. He might well have expected some recognition from the year's Academy Award nominations.

Boston Massachussets. The police are worried by the stranglings of a number of elderly women, apparently the work of a lone maniac. When the strangler turns to younger victims and the case remains unresolved assistant Attorney General John Bottomly is assigned to coordinate the activities of the 'Strangler Bureau' and is aided by tough detective Phil Di Natale. The Bureau follows every lead, interviewing even the unlikeliest suspects, but comes up empty handed. In desperation Bottomly even consults a psychic.

One victim, Dianne Cluny, survives an assault by The Strangler but is so traumatized by the attack that she cannot recall the features of her assailant. All she can tell police is that she bit the man on the hand.

Albert De Salvo, a maintenance man, is arrested after trying to break into an apartment. Happily married, he is a polite, seemingly well-adjusted man who denies the charge despite irrefutable evidence of his guilt. He is transferred to the Boston City Hospital for psychiatric tests. At the hospital human bite marks are observed on his hand. Bottomly suspects that De Salvo is The Strangler but is aware that his mental condition will preclude prosecution. De Salvo is classified as schizophrenic and Bottomly begins

Twentieth Century-Fox

a methodical interrogation designed to make De Salvo admit to himself that he has committed murder. Progress is slow but when De Salvo is visited by his wife he is observed through a two-way mirror as he almost succeeds in strangling her. Subsequently De Salvo breaks down and accepts that he is guilty.

"Tony Curtis plays De Salvo with extraordinary brilliance and sensitivity."

DAILY EXPRESS

"Tony Curtis, with a built-up nose and a baffled expression, managed to move me to feelings of great pity in the final scenes of self-awareness."

SUN

"Under orders from some burning sector of his mind he hysterically re-enacts one killing by wrapping his hands around an imaginary girl's windpipe. Hovering between pathos and terror, Curtis suddenly makes the viewer's breath stop in his own throat."

TIME

TONY CURTIS 117

MONTE CARLO OR BUST

US: THOSE DARING YOUNG MEN IN THEIR JAUNTY JALOPIES

U.S.A.-ITALY-FRANCE 1969 – RUNNING TIME: 125 MINUTES
MARIANNE/MARS/DE LAURENTIIS

DIRECTOR:	KEN ANNAKIN	**CAST**
PRODUCER:	KEN ANNAKIN	
ASSOCIATE PRODUCER:	BASIL KEYS	**TONY CURTIS** — CHESTER SCHOFIELD
SCREENPLAY:	JACK DAVIES	**SUSAN HAMPSHIRE** — BETTY
	AND KEN ANNAKIN	**PETER COOK** — MAJ. DIGBY DAWLISH
ART DIRECTION:	TED HAWORTH	**DUDLEY MOORE** — LT. KIT. BARRINGTON
DIRECTOR OF PHOTOGRAPHY:	GABOR POGANY	**TERRY-THOMAS** — SIR CUTHBERT WARE-ARMITAGE
EDITOR:	PETER TAYLOR	**ERIC SYKES** — PERKINS
SOUND:	JOHN BROMMAGE	**JACK HAWKINS** — COUNT LEVINOVITCH
PRODUCTION SUPERVISORS:	BACCIO BANDINI	**GERT FROBE** — WILLI SCHICKEL/
	AND PETER MANLEY	HORST MULLER
MUSIC:	RON GOODWIN	**BOURVIL** — M. DUPONT
COSTUMES:	JOHN FURNISS	

Ken Annakin had largely been responsible for the success of 'Those Magnificent Men in Their Flying Machines' and 'Monte Carlo or Bust!' was a vain attempt to make lightning strike twice. Filmed between April and October 1968 the production utilised picturesque locations throughout Europe including Monte Carlo, Paris, Stockholm and Visby on the island of Gotland in the Baltic Sea. Interior shots were completed at the Dino De Laurentiis studios in Rome. The film's theme song is performed by Jimmy Durante.

The 1920s. In England Sir Cuthbert Ware Armitage inherits a car factory and plans to produce the 'Nifty Nine'. To his horror he learns that he is only a half-owner, his late father having lost the other half to American gambler Chester Schofield who has his own plans to manufacture the 'Triple S'. Sir Cuthbert, an inveterate cheat, suggests that they enter their respective vehicles in the Monte Carlo Rally and the winner takes all. Sir Cuthbert blackmails his secretary Perkins into being his co-driver and ensures that Chester's partner falls ill. Driving over the English moors Chester meets Betty who stays for the race.

Among the other competitors are British officer Dawlish and Kit Barrington and two German prisoners, Schickel and Otto, who plan to transport stolen jewels across international customs. Three French girls led by Dr. Marie Claude compete but when they stop for a swim their clothes are stolen. Two Italian policemen have invested in a Lancia to enter the Rally. En route Sir Cuthbert tries to blow up a refuelling station but only destroys his own car which he illegally replaces. He manages to drug Chester's glass of milk and, when he falls asleep, Betty takes over the wheel landing them on the edge of a frozen waterfall. Dawlish and Barrington come to the rescue and Marie-Claude gives Chester a 24 hour pep pill. Later Marie-Claude and her team drop out of the race to tend to the injured and the Italians vow to win the trophy and dedicate it to them.

In Monte Carlo the Rally Secretary announces that the Rally will be decided by a race around the Grande Corniche next morning. Dawlish and Barrington's car explodes, Perkins is finally able to report Sir Cuthbert for cheating and he is disqualified, the Germans are arrested and the Italians win the race. Chester has fallen asleep at the wheel and Betty pushes the car over the finishing line. He has defeated Sir Cuthbert and the factory is his. Betty accepts his marriage proposal.

Susan Hampshire   Marianne/Mars/De Laurentiis

"It is a fast and funny film. A lovely effervescent Susan Hampshire plays a bright young thing teamed up with Tony Curtis who pulls out all the comedy stops as an American motormaniac with the versatility of a clever clown."

MORNING STAR

"After the austerity of budget and paucity of taste in so much of the current product the film's unstinting effort to entertain at all costs is both welcome and refreshing."

SATURDAY REVIEW

"Susan Hampshire fits most prettily into the 'Twenties scene and Tony Curtis fools about quite adequately."

SUN

TONY CURTIS 119

SUPPOSE THEY GAVE A WAR AND NOBODY CAME

U.S.A. 1969 – RUNNING TIME: 113 MINUTES
ABC PICTURES CORPORATION

		CAST	
DIRECTOR:	HY AVERBACK		
PRODUCER:	FRED ENGEL		
ASSOCIATE PRODUCER:	J. PAUL POPKIN	TONY CURTIS	SHANNON GAMBRONI
SCREENPLAY:	DON MCGUIRE	BRIAN KEITH	NACE
	AND HAL CAPTAIN	ERNEST BORGNINE	SHERIFF HARVE
ART DIRECTION:	JACK POPLIN	IVAN DIXON	SGT. JONES
DIRECTOR OF PHOTOGRAPHY:	BURNETT GUFFEY	SUZANNE PLESHETTE	RAMONA
EDITOR:	JOHN F. BURNETT	TOM EWELL	BILLY JOE DAVIS
SOUND:	EVERETT HUGHES	BRADFORD DILLMAN	CAPT. MYERSON
PRODUCTION SUPERVISOR:	JOE POPKIN	ARTHUR O'CONNELL	MR KRUFT
MUSIC:	JERRY FIELDING	JOHN FIELDER	MAJOR PURVIS
COSTUMES:	JERRY ALPERT	DON AMECHE	COL. FLANDERS
		BOB EMHARDT	LESTER CALHOUN

'Suppose They Gave a War and Nobody Came' is flawed by its uncertainty as to whether it is comedy or drama, satire or madcap farce. Suzanne Pleshette's character disappears from the film altogether. In isolated moments Curtis can be seen giving his most affecting light comedy performance in years. The climactic chase scene involved some thirty-two used cars and pick-up trucks, two jeeps, several helicopters, over a dozen motorcycles and two tanks. The orgy of automative destruction was overseen by a team of twelve top stuntmen. An inventive mind chose to advertise the film as a 'peacetime MASH' but there were few takers.

In Davis County relations between the local citizenry and the fun-loving members of the nearby Army Base are not good. Warrant Officer Nace is assigned to the Base with orders to improve community relations. At Fort Blair he is reunited with his long-time friends Gambroni and Jones. Middle-age is beginning to catch up on the trio; Nace is teetotal because of a liver complaint, Jones is hoping to leave the army and open a petrol station whilst Gambroni just can't understand the seriousness of the younger generation. The irrepressible Gambroni is interested in 'booze, broads' and restoring an obsolete tank nicknamed 'Moma 2'. When the beautiful Ramona starts work at the base he develops an interest in her too.

Nace's superior, Colonel Flanders, wants to attain the rank of Brigadier before his impending retirement and orders a party for the city dignitaries to improve his community record. The 'dignitaries' include bigoted, right-wing town leader Billy Joe Davis and the sadistic sheriff 'Fat' Harve. On the night of the party Gambroni is arrested by Harve, and Nace, sickened by the toadying to the civilians, becomes increasingly drunk. Later, Harve refuses to give the badly-beaten Gambroni into Jones's custody. Jones returns to the Base and, together with Nace, commandeers 'Moma 2' and heads for Davis County promising to blow the jail sky high. Billy Joe prepares to defend himself from attack and calls up his private army who prove no match for 'Moma 2'. Nace and Jones journey on, break down the jail and free Gambroni, the mayor finally sees sense and fires Harve, and Colonel Flanders arrives to clear up the mess.

ABC Pictures Corporation

"It has one very funny sequence of a horrifying square dance given by the Army to entertain its civilian hosts. Amusing performances too from Tony Curtis, Don Ameche, Brian Keith and Bradford Dillman"

OBSERVER

"Tony Curtis keeps it lighthearted, but nevertheless convincing, as a middle-aged, paunchy garrison soldier who thinks he is Warren Beatty."

VARIETY

YOU CAN'T WIN 'EM ALL

UNITED KINGDOM 1970 – RUNNING TIME: 99 MINUTES
SRO COMPANY

		CAST	
DIRECTOR:	PETER COLLINSON		
PRODUCER:	GENE CORMAN		
ASSOCIATE PRODUCER:	HAROLD BUCK	TONY CURTIS	ADAM DYER
SCREENPLAY:	LEO V. GORDON	CHARLES BRONSON	JOSH COREY
ART DIRECTION:	SEAMUS FLANNERY	MICHELE MERCIER	AILA
DIRECTOR OF PHOTOGRAPHY:	KEN HIGGINS	GREGOIRE ASLAN	OSMAN BEY
EDITOR:	RAYMOND POULTON	FIKRET HAKAN	COL. ELCI
SOUND:	ARTHUR VINCENT	SALIH GUNEY	CAPT. ENVER
PRODUCTION MANAGER:	DEREK PARR	PATRICK MAGEE	THE GENERAL
MUSIC:	BERT KAEMPFERT	TONY BONNER	REESE
COSTUMES:	DINA GREET	JOHN ACHESON	DAVIS
		JOHN ALDERSON	US MAJOR
		HORST JANSEN	WOLLER

Originally planned as a project for veteran adventure director Howard Hawks, 'You Can't Win 'Em All' wound up in the hands of Britisher Peter Collinson whose previous credits included the war film 'The Long Day's Dying' (1968) and the comedy caper 'The Italian Job' (1969).

Based on a script by the character-actor Leo V. Gordon, who also takes a role in the film, production began under the working title of 'The Dubious Patriots'. Filming took place in Turkey, about 200 miles from Istanbul where work proceeded high up in the mountains under the broiling heat of 120 degree temperatures. The film is merely bread and butter escapism but Curtis and Bronson display some engaging team work. Bronson later criticised the director saying; "He can only work in a fraught atmosphere, whipping up everyone against everyone else. This is awful. It was an awful experience for me making You Can't Win 'Em All."

Turkey, 1922. The Ottoman Empire is crumbling as the country is torn apart by civil war. Former American soldiers Adam Dyer and Josh Corey are hired by Osman Bey, a provincial Governor, to accompany an armoured train from the interior to the port city of Smyrna. The train's cargo consists of gold bullion, the Governor's three daughters and their protector — the beautiful Aila.

During the journey Adam discovers that the bullion is really gold-plated lead but Josh uncovers the fact that Aila is in possession of a casket filled with precious jewels. En route to Smyrna the two mercenaries fight off attacks by guerrillas and rival Turkish forces. Arriving in Smyrna they are captured by the rebel forces. When the jewels cannot be found the rebel commander, 'the General', accuses Adam and Josh of theft. Aila intervenes, revealing herself as an agent of the rebels and convinces 'the General' that the jewels have been lost in transit. All is forgiven when it is discovered that Adam and Josh have unwittingly rescued the Koran; the Turkish symbol of power.

Adam and Josh are subsequently expelled from Turkey but leave the country plotting a profitable future as soldiers of fortune.

"Curtis and Bronson occasionally strike a few sparks together, but the going is rough when they are forced to engage in some of the lamest repartee that can ever have passed for wit in an American movie."

THE HOLLYWOOD REPORTER

"You Can't Win 'Em All is both a title and a kind dismissal to this Gene Corman potboiler."

VARIETY

Charles Bronson   SRO Company

LEPKE

U.S.A. 1974 – RUNNING TIME: 110 MINUTES
AMERIEURO PICTURE CORPORATION

		CAST	
DIRECTOR:	MENAHEM GOLAN		
PRODUCER:	MENAHEM GOLAN		
EXECUTIVE PRODUCER:	YORAM GLOBUS	TONY CURTIS	LEPKE
SCREENPLAY:	WESLEY LAU	ANJANETTE COMER	BERNICE
	AND TAMAR HOFFS	MICHAEL CALLAN	KANE
ART DIRECTION:	JACK DEGOVIA	WARREN BERLINGER	GURRAH
DIRECTOR OF PHOTOGRAPHY:	ANDREW DAVIS	GIANNI RUSSO	ANASTASIA
EDITOR:	DOV HOENIG	VIC TAYBACK	LUCIANO
SOUND:	BOB CASEY	MARY WILCOX	MARION
PRODUCTION MANAGER:	LANY GUSTAVSON	JACK ACKERMAN	LITTLE AUGIE
MUSIC:	KEN WANNBERG	LOUIS GUSS	MAX
COSTUMES:	JODIE TILLEN	VAUGHN MEADER	WALTER WINCHELL
		MILTON BERLE	MEYER

Curtis's comeback film was something of a throwback to the gangster films of the 1930s and gave him a worthy dramatic role. He was enthusiastic about leading Israeli filmmaker Menahem Golan saying; 'He's excellent with actors. He has a rapport with them and knows how to provoke them. He lets each actor feel as if they're contributing a specific gift and not just like those little paper dolls you cut out and put clothes on. He's a fine director."

Curtis researched the part thoroughly and was particularly intrigued by the fact that the only mobster to go to the electric chair was Jewish.

1912. Louis 'Lepke' Buchalter begins his life of crime as a petty thief in the streets of New York's . Lower East Side. His father dies when Lepke is 15 and the boy spends his formative years in jail until 1919 when he is released. On the outside he is reunited with two childhood friends — Gurrah Shapiro and Robert Kane. Gurrah introduces him to a vicious gang of strikebreakers and, within a few years, Lepke becomes the head of the mobsters forming the Brooklyn Group, later dubbed Murder Inc. by Walter Winchell. Robert's friendship reflects the respectable side of Lepke's life. Robert, (a struggling lawyer,) becomes Lepke's personal legal adviser and introduces him to young widow Bernice Meyer. Lepke later marries Bernice and adopts her son, much to the disgust of her father.

Over the years Lepke's empire grows and he moves into narcotics. He is responsible for many deaths and also develops enemies within the criminal fraternity. Ambitious district attorney Thomas Dewey manages to indict Lepke on a minor charge. Lepke is enraged and orders the execution of a suspected informant before corroborating witnesses. He is arrested but jumps bail and spends the next two years on the run separated from Bernice. The law turns the mob against Lepke by threatening a massive clamp-down on their activities unless Lepke is surrendered to the authorities. Lepke is tricked into thinking that he has made a deal whereby he need only serve twelve years in jail. However, he stands trial for murder and, despite the efforts of Robert and Bernice, he is electrocuted in 1944, aged 47.

"Lepke, by the strength and sincerity of the central performance by Tony Curtis, is compelling: Curtis convinces us utterly of his ruthlessness and while we don't exactly share his conviction of his immortality, the savage realism of the electric chair climax is quite horrifying."
FILMS ILLUSTRATED

AmeriEuro Picture Corporation

"Brooklyn mob leader Louis 'Lepke' Buchalter is endowed by Tony Curtis with a nice line in compulsive viciousness."

FILMS AND FILMING

"We have been reading a lot in the news recently about the Golan Heights. Consider Lepke a Golan low."

HOLLYWOOD REPORTER

THE COUNT OF MONTE CRISTO

U.S.A. 1974 – RUNNING TIME: 103 MINUTES
NORMAN ROSEMONT PRODUCTION WITH ITC

DIRECTOR:	DAVID GREENE	
PRODUCER:	NORMAN ROSEMONT	
SCREENPLAY:	SIDNEY CARROLL	
	BASED ON THE NOVEL BY	
	ALEXANDRE DUMAS	
ART DIRECTION:	WALTER PATRIARCA	
DIRECTOR OF PHOTOGRAPHY:	ALDO TONTI	
EDITOR:	GENE MILFORD	
PRODUCTION SUPERVISOR:	GIANNI COZZO	
MUSIC:	ALLYN FERGUSON	
COSTUMES:	LUCIANA MARINUCCI	

CAST

RICHARD CHAMBERLAIN	EDMOND DANTES
TONY CURTIS	MONDEGO
TREVOR HOWARD	ABBE FARIA
LOUIS JOURDAN	DE VILLEFORT
DONALD PLEASENCE	DANGLARS
KATE NELLIGAN	MERCEDES
ANGELO INFANTI	JACOPO
TARYN POWER	VALENTINE DE VILLEFORT
HAROLD BROMLEY	M.MORRELL
CARLO PURI	ANDREA BENEDETTO

Originally made for American television 'The Count of Monte Cristo' was released to cinemas in other parts of the world and finally appeared on British screens in 1976. Alexandre Dumas' story had first been filmed in 1912 and, over the years, his vengeance-seeking hero has been impersonated by the likes of John Gilbert, Louis Jourdan and, most famously, Robert Donat. Officially this was the seventh screen version and certainly does nothing to erase fond memories of the 1934 Donat classic. Chamberlain makes a competent romantic figure but the crossing of swords is very tamely executed. To please his young family Curtis had wanted to return to the swashbucklers of his youth before he was too old.

Following a visit by his captain to Napoleon on the island of Elba, ship's officer Edmond Dantes is entrusted with a letter to deliver. On shore Dantes is denounced as a Bonapartist by two of his crew and Mondego, the cousin of his fiancee Mercedes. He surrenders the letter to the prosecutor De Villefort and is consigned to the island prison Chateau d'If for his troubles. Unknown to Dantes the letter was intended for De Villefort's father, an infamous Bonapartist and an embarrassment to the ambitious prosecutor.

Dantes spends ten years incarcerated until he is joined by Abbe Faria, a fellow prisoner who has arrived in his cell whilst attempting to dig an escape tunnel. The two become friends and Dantes learns much from the old man including the location of a treasure trove on the island of Monte Cristo. When Faria dies Dantes conceals himself in the burial sack and is thrown into the sea. He is rescued by a band of smugglers and, together, they recover the treasure. Dantes now calls himself the Count of Monte Cristo and sets about revenging himself on those who betrayed him.

The sailor Caderousse is killed in a fight with a young man, Fautino, who has been hired by Dantes. Dantes provides the evidence that enables Faustino to ruin De Villefort and former officer Danglars who commits suicide when made bankrupt. The last name on his list is Mondego, now married to Mercedes and a respected military hero. Dantes exposes Mondego as a cheat and a murderer and defeats him in a duel after which Mondego is arrested. Having extracted his vengeance Dantes bids farewell to Mercedes who leaves to be with her son.

Norman Rosemont Productions/ITC

"Tony Curtis proves an interestingly aberrant, huskily Brooklyn choice as the naughty general, Mondego."

NEW STATESMAN

"Nastier roles are played with varying degrees of conviction by Louis Jourdan, Donald Pleasence and Tony Curtis, who shouldn't be asked to do this kind of stuff any more; his disbelief has been too much suspended already."

OBSERVER

"Richard Chamberlain looks as though he could give a good account of the title role if only the director would help a bit. Tony Curtis is appalling as Mondego."

FILMS ILLUSTRATED

THE LAST TYCOON

U.S.A. 1976 – RUNNING TIME: 123 MINUTES
ACADEMY PICTURES A.G. PRODUCTION

		CAST	
DIRECTOR:	ELIA KAZAN		
PRODUCER:	SAM SPIEGEL		
SCREENPLAY:	HAROLD PINTER FROM THE NOVEL	ROBERT DE NIRO	MONROE STAHR
	BY F. SCOTT FITZGERALD	TONY CURTIS	RODRIGUEZ
ART DIRECTION:	GENE CALLAHAN	ROBERT MITCHUM	PAT BRADY
DIRECTOR OF PHOTOGRAPHY:	VICTOR KEMPERER	JEANNE MOREAU	DIDI
EDITOR:	RICHARD MARKS	JACK NICHOLSON	BRIMMER
SOUND:	LARRY JOST	DONALD PLEASENCE	BOXLEY
PRODUCTION MANAGER:	LLOYD ANDERSON	INGRID BOULTING	KATHLEEN MOORE
MUSIC:	MAURICE JARRE	RAY MILLAND	FLEISHACKLER
COSTUMES:	ANNA HILL JOHNSTONE	DANA ANDREWS	RED RIDINGWOOD
		THERESA RUSSELL	CECILIA BRADY
		PETER STRAUSS	WYLIE

Veteran producer Sam Spiegel, responsible for 'The African Queen' (1952) and 'Lawrence of Arabia' (1962), spent many years attempting to bring the last, uncompleted novel of F. Scott Fitzgerald to the screen. Fitzgerald had died in 1940 before finishing his portrait of tinsel-town and a film mogul generally held to be Irving Thalberg. Spiegel first announced the project in June 1973 naming Mike Nichols as director. Eventually the four million pound enterprise went before the cameras in October 1975 with Elia Kazan, director of 'Streetcar Named Desire' (1951) and 'On the Waterfront' (1954), at the helm. De Niro, Boulting and Russell underwent extensive rehearsals and Kazan, working on his final film, maintained a policy of no visitors to the set throughout filming.

Fitzgerald's novel had previously been dramatised for American television in 1957 with a cast headed by Jack Palance, Lee Remick and Peter Lorre. John Frankenheimer was the director.

Hollywood in the 1930s. Powerful 'production genius' Monroe Stahr is totally absorbed by work as he continues to mourn his late wife, screen star Mina Davis. His studio has just announced profits of $27 million but Stahr is an isolated figure, coping with other peoples' jealousies and insecurities. Temperamental actress Didi is worried about her fading beauty, screen lover Rodriguez feels that his marriage and image are threatened by his impotence, studio head Pat Brady believes that Stahr is taking all the credit for his hard work, whilst Brady's daughter Cecilia is annoyed that Stahr shows no interest in her.

One evening, during an earthquake, Stahr catches a glimpse of the lovely Kathleen Moore who reminds him of his wife. He is bewitched by Kathleen and uses the resources of the studio to discover where she lives. The two meet and renew acquaintance at the Screenwriter's Ball. Kathleen reluctantly agrees to accompany him to the site of his new mansion on the coast. By now Stahr is infatuated by the mysterious Kathleen and the couple make love. Later however he receives a letter stating that Kathleen is to be married. He persists in his demand to meet her again and the couple arrange a weekend together. At the last moment a telegram is delivered to Stahr informing him that Kathleen is now married.

Totally dejected Stahr goes to dinner with Cecilia and Brimmer, a Communist negotiator from New York who is attempting to unionise the writers in Hollywood. Stahr becomes drunk and tries to strike Brimmer but is knocked to the ground. Brady seizes on the incident to have Stahr declared incompetent and gains control of the studio. Stahr is ordered to take a long rest.

Academy Pictures A. G. Productions

"Tony Curtis, whose own screen career has shown how to climb hand-over-hand from pretty boy to middle-aged character actor, turns in a concentrated, highly self-critical portrait of an Errol Flynn superstar with hardening arteries."

SUNDAY TIMES

"Tony Curtis, let it be said, also has his moments of relishable interest as the stud-star gone twitchily impotent."

NEW STATESMAN

Casanova & Co.

UK TITLE: THE RISE AND RISE OF CASANOVA

AUSTRIAN-FRENCH-ITALIAN-W.GERMAN CO-PRODUCTION 1977 –
RUNNING TIME: 101 MINUTES
NEUE DELTA FILM/PANTHER FILM/COFCI/TV13

		CAST	
DIRECTOR:	FRANCOIS LEGRAND (FRANZ ANTEL)		
PRODUCER:	FRANZ ANTEL		
	AND CARL SZOKOLL	TONY CURTIS	GIACOMO CASANOVA/
SCREENPLAY:	JOSHUA SINCLAIR		GIACOMINO
	AND TOM PRIMAN	MARISA BERENSON	CALIPHA OF SHIRAZ
ART DIRECTION:	NINO BORGHI	HUGH GRIFFITH	CALIPH OF SHIRAZ
DIRECTOR OF PHOTOGRAPHY:	HANNS MATULA	MARISA MELL	DUCHESS FRANCESCA
EDITOR:	MICHEL LEWIN	BRITT EKLAND	COUNTESS TRIVULZI
SOUND:	WALTER PROKOSCH	JEAN LEFEBVRE	SERGEANT
PRODUCTION SUPERVISOR:	GEORGE GLASS	ANDREA FERREOLE	BEATRICE
MUSIC:	RIZ ORTOLANI	SYLVIA KOSCINA	GELSOMINA
COSTUMES:	HELGA BANDINI	VICTOR SPINETTI	PREFECT

'Casanova & Co.' was filmed on a budget of $2,331,000 in Venice during the late Summer of 1976. One scene was filmed at the city's annual historical regatta on the Grand Canal and the schedule was so concentrated that Curtis was unable to attend the local Film Festival of that year. Interviewed during the production by Variety, Curtis admitted that he was attracted to the film for two reasons: a very funny script and money. Apart from the flat fee for his services Curtis was on a percentage of the film's takings in America and Canada which he would receive 'from the first dollar' that the film grossed.

Curtis appears in drag in the film, the first such occasion since his memorable role in 'Some Like It Hot', and, in some areas, the Casanova film was released as 'Some Like It Cool' in a fruitless attempt to exploit the connection for commercial gain.

Venice, 1756. The Caliph of Shiraz arrives in town to complete negotiations for a rose oil contract with Senator Dell'Acqua. The Calipha demands that the famous Casanova make love to her as one of the conditions of the contract. Dell'Acqua is unable to provide this service as Casanova has escaped from the custody of the authorities along with his double, the pickpocket Giacomino.

Throughout the city Giacomino is mistaken for Casanova and he makes love to Beatrice, a baker's wife, and Gelsomina, wife of the prefect of police. Meanwhile Casanova has taken refuge in a nunnery where he discovers that he is impotent. Casanova escapes from the city disguised as a monk whilst Giacomino also manages to flee from Venice in the guise of a lady's maid. Both men decide to rest at the same wayside inn but Casanova changes identities with Count Tiretta who is arrested in his place. Casanova heads for the country estate of Countess Trivulzi and a passionate reunion with his beloved Francesca who restores his virility.

Casanova learns of Giacomino's impersonation but it is the latter who is arrested by the bumbling police force and taken to satisfy the Calipha. Giacomino subsequently finds himself impotent but Casanova rushes to the scene and satisfies the Calipha whilst Giacomino plays backgammon with the Caliph. Using a loaded dice Giacomino wins half the Caliph's vast fortune.

Marisa Berenson   Neue Delta Film/Panther Film/COFCI/TV 13

"The film might be able to please an unassuming audience which would be content with a
senseless jumble of a twin Curtis, mild smut and an overdose of (admittedly) beautiful bare bosoms
of every imaginable size."

VARIETY

"As if to underline how far Tony Curtis's career has declined from the heyday of 'Some Like It
Hot', he is requested not only to parade in unconvincing drag but even to repeat the 'nobody's
perfect' punchline."

MONTHLY FILM BULLETIN

THE MANITOU

U.S.A. 1977 – RUNNING TIME: 104 MINUTES
MANITOU PRODUCTIONS

		CAST	
DIRECTOR:	WILLIAM GIRDLER		
PRODUCER:	WILLIAM GIRDLER		
EXECUTIVE PRODUCER:	MELVIN G. GORDY	TONY CURTIS	HARRY ERSKINE
SCREENPLAY:	WILLIAM GIRDLER, JON CEDAR	MICHAEL ANSARA	SINGING ROCK
	AND THOMAS POPE FROM THE NOVEL	SUSAN STRASBERG	KAREN TANDY
	BY GRAHAM MASTERTON	STELLA STEVENS	AMELIA CRUSOE
ART DIRECTION:	WALTER SCOTT HERNDON	JON CEDAR	DR. JACK HUGHES
DIRECTOR OF PHOTOGRAPHY:	MICHEL HUGO	ANN SOTHERN	MRS. KARMANN
EDITOR:	BUB ASMAN	BURGESS MEREDITH	DR. ERNEST SNOW
SOUND:	FRED BROWN	PAUL MANTEE	DR. ROBERT MCEVOY
	AND MICHELLE SHARP BROWN	JEANETTE NOLAN	MRS. WINCONIS
PRODUCTION MANAGER:	GILLES DE TURENNE	LURENE TUTTLE	MRS. HERTZ
MUSIC:	LALO SCHIFRIN		
COSTUMES:	AGNES LYON		
	AND MICHAEL FAETH		

Fantasy specialist William Girdler had already made 'Three on a Meathook' (1973), 'Grizzly' (1976) and 'Day of the Animals' (1977) before coming to the rather ludicrous material of The Manitou. Filming began on a three million dollar budget in San Francisco on May 17th 1977 and proceeded for the next ten weeks. Given the public appetite for 'The Exorcist' (1973) and 'The Omen' (1976), 'The Manitou' at least displayed the potential for box-office success. However, the plotline is too far-fetched and the special effects are generally poor. Even in such unpromising circumstances Curtis contributes an engaging and amiable performance.

Girdler was killed in a helicopter crash on January 21st 1978, aged thirty, whilst scouting locations for a new film in the Philippines.

San Francisco. Karen Tandy is worried by a tumour on the back of her neck which is growing rapidly. She visits Dr. Hughes who is baffled by the case but orders surgery for the following day. Karen seeks reassurance in the company of her former boyfriend, fake mystic and fortune teller, Harry Erskine. In the middle of the night Harry is awakened by Karen chanting a strange Red Indian phrase.

The next day the operation is disrupted when Dr. Hughes becomes strangely transfixed and begins to slash his own wrist. At the same time one of Harry's clients, Mrs Hertz, breaks into an Indian chant and levitates before falling down a flight of stairs to her death. Harry concludes that black magic is at work and meets retired spiritualist Amelia Crusoe to arrange a seance. At the seance the chant is repeated and the skull of a Red Indian appears. Harry and Amelia consult occult expert Dr. Snow who translates the chant as 'my death foretells my return'. Harry now believes that an old piece of folklore has come true and that Karen is about to give birth to the evil spirit of a 400-year-old Red Indian medicineman. Harry's only hope is to find a modern-day medicine-man who will fight for Karen's life. Eventually he persuades John Singing Rock to take the case.

At the hospital the evil spirit is born fully-formed and invokes many demons in his clash with the 'good medicine' of Singing Rock. It is only when the power of the hospital generators is channelled through Karen and combined with the strength of Harry's love that the spirit is defeated.

Michael Ansara   Manitou Productions

"Apart from Meredith's nicely restrained (for once) cameo, only Curtis comes out well. It's a fine part for him at this time and place in his career, and he acts the puffy, weary charlatan with ease. The part is the perfect aged crystallization of what seemed to lie beneath all his frenetically overplayed, Universal swashbuckling heroes of the early '50s."

CINE FANTASTIQUE

"It is difficult to know whether we are supposed to giggle or shiver at the turn of events, since Tony Curtis, as Karen's psychic Tarot-dealing man friend, plays rather entertainingly for laughs the whole way through. Even a sci-fi climax, which I won't give away, has him still cracking jokes."

COSMOPOLITAN

SEXTETTE

U.S.A. 1977 – RUNNING TIME: 91 MINUTES
BRIGGS AND SULLIVAN

		CAST	
DIRECTOR:	KEN HUGHES		
PRODUCER:	DANIEL BRIGGS		
	AND ROBERT SULLIVAN	MAE WEST	MARLO MANNERS
ASSOCIATE PRODUCER:	HARRY WEISS	TIMOTHY DALTON	SIR MICHAEL BARRINGTON
SCREENPLAY:	HERBERT BAKER FROM	DOM DE LUISE	DAN
	THE PLAY BY MAE WEST	TONY CURTIS	ALEXEI
ART DIRECTION:	THAD PRESCOTT	RINGO STARR	LASLO
DIRECTOR OF PHOTOGRAPHY:	JAMES CRABE	GEORGE HAMILTON	WAITER
EDITOR:	ARGYLE NELSON	ALICE COOPER	WAITER
MUSIC:	ARTIE BUTLER	KEITH MOON	DRESS DESIGNER
COSTUMES:	EDITH HEAD	WALTER PIDGEON	CHAIRMAN
		GEORGE RAFT	HIMSELF
		RONA BARRETT	HERSELF
		GIL STRATTON	HIMSELF

Disregarding her brief participation in 'Myra Breckinridge' (1970), 'Sextette' marked Mae West's first major film work in over thirty years and only her twelfth feature. "Some people make 300 pictures and you can't name one of them", she purred defensively in one interview. The redoubtable octogenarian was somewhat sensitive to the age of her leading man and she rejected Paul Newman, Christopher Plummer, Peter Ustinov and Vincent Price as projected co-stars. When Curtis first encountered the legendary lady she asked if he intended to wear a wig to cover his bald patch, only later on did the two become friends.

The two young producers used an inheritance to finance the $3 million independent production of which $250,000 went to Mae West who also received 20% of the film's gross takings. The frail Miss West received a daily, temporary face-lift and her dialogue was conveyed to her through a radio receiver in her left ear that was hidden by a wig. It was reported that she once picked up the signals from a police helicopter and began reporting traffic conditions on the Hollywood Freeway.

Sextette was shown at the 1978 Berlin Film Festival and by-passed British cinemas to be released solely on video in 1982.

London. The honeymoon plans of sex-goddess Marlo Manners and her sixth husband Sir Michael Barrington are continually disrupted by over-inquisitive journalists, rowdy fans and the attentions of Marlo's ex-husbands. Matters are not helped when Marlo's personal manager Dan Turner promises the American Secret Service that Marlo will use her many charms to convince Soviet diplomat Alexei Karansky to withdraw his veto of an international Security Treaty.

Sir Michael is constantly frustrated by the interruptions from Marlo's former spouses, among them middle-European film director Laslo Karolny, young actor Ronald Cartwright, and the hoodlum Vancce who is officially listed as deceased.

During all this activity Marlo loses possession of a cassette tape on which she has recorded the memoirs of her many love affairs. A frantic search begins but Marlo traces the tape to her hotel gymnasium where she encounters an American athletics team. Later Marlo begins her pursuit of Alexei and charms him into voting 'yes' at the Security Council meeting.

Marlo returns to the bridal suite at her hotel but finds that Sir Michael has run off, seemingly

Briggs and Sullivan

disappointed by his bride's continual preoccupation with other matters. Marlo follows him to his yacht and discovers that, in his capacity as a British secret agent, he has been following her every move with Alexei. Happily reunited, the couple settle down to finally consummating their marriage.

"Sextette is one of those movies rarely seen these days, a work so bad, so ferally innocent, that it is good, an instant classic to be treasued by connoisseurs of the genre everywhere."

TIME

"One of the most innocently perverse star vehicles ever made. Sextette is a cult item not only for Mae West devotees but for bad movie aficionados as well."

VILLAGE VOICE

THE BAD NEWS BEARS GO TO JAPAN

U.S.A. 1978 - RUNNING TIME: 91 MINUTES
PARAMOUNT PRODUCTION

		CAST	
DIRECTOR:	JOHN BERRY		
PRODUCER:	MICHAEL RITCHIE		
ASSOCIATE PRODUCER:	TERRY CARR	TONY CURTIS	MARVIN
SCREENPLAY:	BILL LANCASTER	JACKIE EARLE HALEY	KELLY
ART DIRECTION:	WALTER SCOTT HERNDON	TOMISABURO WAKAYAMA	COACH
DIRECTOR OF PHOTOGRAPHY:	GENE POLITO	HATSUNE ISHIHARA	ARIKA
	AND KOZO OKAZAKI	GEORGE WYNER	NETWORK DIRECTOR
EDITOR:	RICHARD A. HARRIS	LONNY CHAPMAN	GAMBLER
SOUND:	GENE CANTAMESA	MATTHEW DOUGLAS ANTON	E.R.W. TILLYARD III
MUSIC:	PAUL CHIHARA	ERIN BLUNT	AHMAD
COSTUMES:	TOMMY WELSH	GEORGE GONZALES	MIGUEL
	AND NANCY MARTINELLI	BRETT MARX	JIMMY
		DAVID POLLOCK	RUDY

'The Bad News Bears' starring Walter Matthau and Tatum O'Neal had been one of the surprise hits of 1976, adding some thirty five million dollars to the coffers of Paramount. A sequel followed, 'The Bad News Bears in Breaking Training' with William Devane, which also proved popular and thus a third 'Bears' film was quickly rushed into production in September 1977. As with the first 'Bears' film the script came from the pen of Bill Lancaster, son of actor Burt Lancaster. The film was partially shot on locations in Japan and went on to become a modest hit grossing around seven million dollars. It was also Curtis's only leading role for a major Hollywood studio since 'The Boston Strangler' ten years previously.

Hollywood agent Marvin Lazar is down on his luck. He has problems with alimony payments to his ex-wife and a debt which he must make good or else face unpleasant consequences. He hits on the get-rich-quick scheme of promoting a baseball game between the misfit Bad News Bears and the Japanese all-star Little Leaguers.

The Bears, a group of players that other teams are proud not to possess, are resistant to the smooth-talking charms of Lazar but dutifully head for The Land of the Rising Sun. In Japan one of the Bears, Kelly, falls in love with Arika and the other team members land Lazar in plenty of trouble. Lazar carries on a rivalry with the Japanese coach and becomes involved in an exhibition wrestling match which all goes to show to the Bears that he is a good sport.

Lazar hustles them into a major baseball fixture at Tokyo's Kawasaki Stadium as the team's final match. A much put upon TV sports director tries tries to capture the match for the audience in America and, ultimately, he announces the Bears as the winners. The Bears are proud of their victory whilst Lazar's scheme has worked and he is able to extricate himself from his financial problems. Along the way Lazar and the Bears have become good friends and, at the end of their Japanese adventures, Marvin asks; 'Where shall we go next year? Cuba!'

"Curtis - more than the Bears - is given center stage and it's the best role the actor has had in several seasons: fast talking, constantly harassed, trying to find a pot of gold before he turns to seed."

HOLLYWOOD REPORTER

Paramount Production

"Latest version is more successful than the middle outing, but the situations and characters are getting tired. What was once fresh and original is now very familiar and even Curtis's energetic performance can't help turn the tide."

VARIETY

IT RAINED ALL NIGHT THE DAY I LEFT

FRANCE-CANADA-ISRAEL CO-PRODUCTION 1979 – RUNNING TIME: 95 MINUTES
COFCI (PARIS)-CANEARUM FILMS INC. (CANADA)-ISRAEL FILMS LTD.

		CAST	
DIRECTOR:	NICOLAS GESSNER		
PRODUCERS:	SHOLOMO MOGRABI		
	AND CLAUDE GIROUX	TONY CURTIS	ROBERT TALBOT
ASSOCIATE PRODUCERS:	LEON ZURATAS	LOUIS GOSSETT JR.	LEO GARCIA
	AND CHRISTOPHE HARBONVILLE	SALLY KELLERMAN	COLONEL
SCREENPLAY:	TED ALLAN FROM AN ORIGINAL	JOHN VERNON	GEORGE KILLIAN
	STORY BY RICHARD WINCKLER	LISA LANGLOIS	SUSSAN
ART DIRECTION:	WOLF KROEGER	GUY HOFFMAN	PRIEST
DIRECTOR OF PHOTOGRAPHY:	RICHARD CIUPKA	WILLIAM CLARKSON	JOMMO
EDITOR:	YVES LANGLOIS	BERTRAND A. HENRY	BOURO
SOUND:	PATRICK ROUSSEAU	GABY AMRANY	WEASEL
PRODUCTION MANAGER:	NISSIM LEVY		
MUSIC:	ALAIN J. LEROUX		
COSTUMES:	JENEPHER HOOPER		

The cumbersomely titled 'It Rained All Night The Day I Left' was the first film to be made under a Canadian-Israeli co-production treaty signed between the two countries on the occasion of the Canadian Secretary of State John Roberts' visit to Israel in March 1978. Other than that there is precious little of interest that can be said. In Britain the film did not receive a cinema release and went straight on to video.

The majority of the five million dollar budget came from Canada. Principal photography began on October 17th and, after three weeks at the Sonolab Studios in Montreal, the unit moved to Israel and was based fifteen kilometres from Eilat until just before Christmas 1978. Given the often turbulent state of Israel's relations with her neighbours the Israeli government arranged war risk insurance to cover the cast, crew sets and equipment. In an 1979 interview Curtis said; "It was a thoroughly inept operation. And I'm too old to put up with that kind of thing."

Adventurers Robert Talbot and Leo Garcia have turned to gun-running for their latest enterprise. In the middle of the African desert they are ambushed by two men who drive off with the guns and are subsequently ambushed themselves; one is killed and one survives. Talbot and Garcia discover the survivor who leads them to the property of the 'Colonel'.

The 'Colonel' is in fact dead, his widow Agnes having remained to carry on his work along with their 19-year-old daughter Sussan. Agnes explains how her husband had bought territory in the old days of colonialism, found the only water and worked the land. They had chosen to stay on after black independence and her husband was murdered. In revenge she has cut off the water supply, and now nothing grows.

Talbot and Garcia are hired to protect the water pump which is turned on twice a day, giving a meagre ration to the natives and her rival George Killian. Killian attempts a business marriage with Agnes which does not transpire. He takes control of the water pump but, after dark, Talbot and Garcia stage a raid and win back Agnes's ownership.

Garcia and Agnes now plan to marry whilst Sussan has grown attracted to Talbot. Talbot is frustrated by Agnes's bitterness which deprives the natives of a water supply which is rightfully theirs. After one argument he leaves with Susan but they are both kidnapped by Killian. At the wedding Killian offers

Louis Gossett Jr.   Cofci-Canearum-Israel Films Ltd

Sussan's life for control of the water. However, Talbot comes to the rescue, freeing everyone, but not before he has given the natives guns and control of the water. A decree of land nationalisation has ended the 'Colonel's' dominance. Talbot and Garcia head into the desert for further adventures.

"Tony Curtis, Louis Gossett et Sally Kellerman animent avec brio cette comédie qui dose avec goût les gags et l'action, l'étude des caractères at les péripéties inattendues. Un excellent divertisement et l'occasion de retrouver Tony Curtis au mieux de sa forme dans un rôle qui lui va comme un gant."

CINE REVUE

TITLE SHOT

CANADA 1979 – RUNNING TIME: 83 MINUTES
REGENTHALL FILM PRODUCTIONS

		CAST	
DIRECTOR:	LES ROSE		
PRODUCER:	ROB IVESON		
EXECUTIVE PRODUCER:	RICHARD GABOURIE	TONY CURTIS	FRANK RENZETTI
SCREENPLAY:	JOHN SAXTON FROM AN	RICHARD GABOURIE	BLAKE
	ORIGINAL IDEA BY RICHARD GABOURIE	SUSAN HOGAN	SYLVIA
ART DIRECTION:	KAREN BROMLEY	ALLAN ROYAL	DUNLOP
DIRECTOR OF PHOTOGRAPHY:	HENRI FIKS	ROBERT DELBERT	RUFUS TAYLOR
EDITOR:	RONALD SANDERS	NATSUKO OHAMA	TERRY
SOUND:	PETER BURGESS	JACK DUFFY	MR GREEN
PRODUCTION MANAGER:	IAN MCDOUGALL	SEAN MCCANN	LT. GRACE
MUSIC:	PAUL JAMES ZAZA	TABORAH JOHNSON	CONNIE ROSE
COSTUMES:	LINDA MATHESON	ROBERT O'REE	IGGY
		DENNIS STRONG	EDDIE

Curtis's second Canadian film in a row managed to be as undistinguished as his previous outing. The film was made on a tight budget (one million, four hundred thousand dollars) by a relatively inexperienced team that encountered financial and union problems during production. Curtis added a touch of professional gloss to the venture and picked up one hundred and fifty thousand dollars for just over a fortnight's work. He had only agreed to make the film after eight months of negotiations with his then agent Irving Lazar.

Director Les Rose said; "Working with Tony was a valuable learning experience. It was a give and take situation. We developed a rapport that took us through the whole picture. It was a 50-50 proposition. Tony is a lot like a fine sports car. If you treat it well it will perform better than anything in the field."

The film received its premiere at the Toronto Festival of Festivals in 1979 and only appeared on video in Britain.

Toronto. Frank Renzetti, ruthless crime boss and fight promoter, arrives in town to manage the latest title defence of world heavyweight boxing champion Rufus Taylor. In secrecy he meets Mr Green to persuade him to provide the bankroll of $5,000,000 to place a bet on Taylor's opponent Nicky Romano, the underdog in the contest. From his various sources of information Renzetti senses that Taylor is on his way out and that Romano will win. Renzetti owns Romano and aims to make a fortune from the good odds he can obtain. Mr Green gives him the money and expects to gain; otherwise Renzetti will die.

In charge of security at the champ's training camp is detective Blake, a man who has long wanted to see Renzetti behind bars. When Taylor breaks training to visit his girlfriend, singer Conny Rose, there is an attempt on his life and Connie is wounded. Blake wants to cancel the fight but Renzetti insists that it go ahead as planned. When there is a second failed attempt to kill Taylor Blake becomes suspicious. He surmises that someone is out to frighten the champ and disrupt his concerted efforts to retain the title. Blake attempts to discover who is behind Coxswill Investments, a mysterious company listed as owning Romano.

At the ringside Renzetti has provided his own insurance against a Taylor victory; a concealed marksman ready to fire on his command. Initially Romano seems certain to win on points but when

Regenthall Film Productions

Taylor gains the upper hand Renzetti signals that he be shot. Meanwhile, Blake has discovered that Renzetti owns Coxswill Investments and Romano. In the arena he seeks out the sniper and, in an exchange of shots, kills him. Taylor knocks out Romano and retains the title. Renzetti is ushered from the arena to face Mr Green.

"The film itself (is) bogged down by unclear explanation of who the principal players are (notably Tony Curtis, a ring owner who sells the attempted kill to a Mafia chieftain) and dialog that appears to border on outright comedy, though unintentionally. Acting, except for Curtis, was slow."

VARIETY

LITTLE MISS MARKER

U.S.A. 1980 – RUNNING TIME: 112 MINUTES
UNIVERSAL

		CAST	
DIRECTOR:	WALTER BERNSTEIN		
PRODUCER:	JENNINGS LANG		
EXECUTIVE PRODUCER:	WALTER MATTHAU	WALTER MATTHAU	SORROWFUL JONES
SCREENPLAY:	WALTER BERNSTEIN FROM A STORY	JULIE ANDREWS	AMANDA
	BY DAMON RUNYON	TONY CURTIS	BLACKIE
ART DIRECTION:	EDWARD C. CARFAGNO	BOB NEWHART	REGRET
DIRECTOR OF PHOTOGRAPHY:	PHILIP LATHROP	LEE GRANT	THE JUDGE
EDITOR:	EVE NEWMAN	SARA STIMSON	'THE KID'
SOUND:	JOHN CARTER	BRIAN DENNEHY	HERBIE
PRODUCTION MANAGER:	DONALD ROBERTS	KENNETH MCMILLAN	BRANNIGAN
MUSIC:	HENRY MANCINI	ANDREW RUBIN	CARTER
COSTUMES:	RUTH MORLEY	JOSHUA SHELLEY	BENNY
		RANDY HERMAN	CLERK
		NEDRA VOLZ	MRS CLANCY

A fourth version of Damon Runyon's classic, 'Little Miss Marker', seemed an ideal vehicle for the grouchy comic persona of Walter Matthau. The star had long wanted to make the film and was quoted as saying; "Sorrowful Jones was made to order for me. This is classic sceptical hard-bitten experience versus love and innocence and how love and innocence wins." Gifted screenwriter Walter Bernstein made his debut as a director with a production which filmed at Curtis's former home studio Universal and on diverse California locations including the Sonoma County Fair-ground, the Long Beach Amusement Park and the Los Angeles County Museum of Natural History. During filming Bernstein said; "Tony Curtis is just wonderful. I think Tony has gotten better and better as an actor as he's gotten older. He is complicated and he's funny and he belongs. He and Walter Matthau together are a very good mix."

Despite the top talent involved the film was not a success, much to the chagrin of Matthau.

New York, the 1930s. Mean-spirited bookmaker Sorrowful Jones is persuaded by one customer to accept his daughter as a guarantee against his bet, when he does not return Sorrowful is lumbered with 'the Kid'. The same day Sorrowful is made an offer he can't refuse by local gangster Blackie — $50,000 in return for a half share in a casino.

Sorrowful visits the site of the casino — a country mansion owned by socialite Amanda who has fallen on hard times. Later Sorrowful takes 'the Kid' to the races to watch Amanda's thoroughbred Sir Galahad who finishes last. The trio spend the day at Coney Island and Amanda senses a warmth beneath Sorrowful's gruff exterior. When Sorrowful learns that 'the Kid's' father has killed himself he decides to look after her permanently.

At the casino one customer hits a winning streak and bankrupts Blackie who blames Sorrowful for insisting that he runs a legitimate operation. Blackie decides to enter Sir Galahad in a race at 40-1 and drug the horse so that it comes first; he will recoup his money but the horse is certain to die. Sorrowful knows this will upset Amanda so he bribes all the other jockeys to allow Sir Galahad to win. Unfortunately the horse is disqualified, Blackie wants his money and Amanda thinks that Sorrowful is a cheat. To pacify Blackie Sorrowful promises him his bookmaking operation. When the police find the little girl Sorrowful rushes to a court hearing to find himself competing with Amanda for custody of the child. The two choose to marry and provide a proper home for 'the Kid'.

Universal

"This time Walter Matthau is the bookie and his unblinking sour-sweet charm acceptably disinfects the story's sentimentality. So does Tony Curtis's splendid Blackie, a light-hearted sketch of a vicious crook which, coming after Curtis's brilliant performance as David Selznick on TV in Moviola, suggests that he has attained maturity as a performer."

CATHOLIC HERALD

THE MIRROR CRACK'D

UNITED KINGDOM 1980 - RUNNING TIME: 105 MINUTES
GW FILMS LTD

DIRECTOR:	GUY HAMILTON	CAST
PRODUCER:	JOHN BRABOURNE	
	AND RICHARD GOODWIN	ANGELA LANSBURY ... MISS MARPLE
SCREENPLAY:	JONATHAN HALES	GERALDINE CHAPLIN ... ELLA ZIELINSKY
	AND BARRY SANDLER FROM THE BOOK	TONY CURTIS ... MARTY N. FENN
	BY AGATHA CHRISTIE	EDWARD FOX ... INSPECTOR CRADDOCK
ART DIRECTION:	MICHAEL STRINGER	ROCK HUDSON ... JASON RUDD
DIRECTOR OF PHOTOGRAPHY:	CHRISTOPHER CHALLIS	KIM NOVAK ... LOLA BREWSTER
EDITOR:	RICHARD MARDEN	ELIZABETH TAYLOR ... MARINA RUDD
SOUND:	JOHN MITCHELL, BILL ROWE	WENDY MORGAN ... CHERRY
	AND JOHN RICHARDS	MARGARET COURTENAY ... MRS BANTRY
PRODUCTION MANAGER:	JIM BRENNAN	CHARLES GRAY ... BATES
MUSIC:	JOHN CAMERON	
COSTUMES:	PHYLLIS DALTON	

Producers John Brabourne and Richard Goodwin had been responsible for the widely popular series of films featuring Agatha Christie's detective Hercule Poirot — initiated in 1974 with 'Murder on the Orient Express'. The intention with 'The Mirror Crack'd' was to commence a similar series around the exploits of Christie's Miss Marple, previously played on screen by Margaret Rutherford. To date no series has developed despite Angela Lansbury's splendid Home Counties' sleuth. The film, although modestly successful, was considered a disappointment at the box-office. Intent on using stars of the 'Fifties Natalie Wood was announced for a leading role, but instead Elizabeth Taylor emerged from her self-imposed retirement.

The five million pound production began its ten weeks of filming on May 12th 1980 and finished on July 18th having survived the worst Kent summer since 1907. Locations used included the Tudor village of Smarden and a two thousand acre private estate near Wrotham in Kent. Twickenham Studios provided the base for the interior scenes.

England, 1953. In the quiet village of St. Mary's Mead Hollywood star Marina Gregg is about to embark on her comeback film following a long absence from the screen. Marina and her husband Jason Rudd, the film's director, appear at the village Coronation fete attended by amateur sleuth Jane Marple and starstruck villager Heather Babcock.

During the festivities Marina is cornered by Heather who reminds her of a previous meeting during the War — Heather had braved illness to kiss her favourite star backstage at a troop show. In the middle of this story Marina is suddenly thunderstruck, her gaze transfixed by a portrait of the Madonna and Child. The episode is quickly forgotten with the arrival of brash film producer Marty Fenn and his wife Lola Brewster. However, soon afterwards Heather collapses and dies, her drink poisoned.

Incapacitated by a fall Miss Marple learns of the events from her cleaner Cherry who recalls that Heather had drunk from a glass intended for Marina. When Marina narrowly escapes drinking the contents of a poisoned cup of coffee it is assumed that someone is trying to murder her. Miss Marple's nephew, Inspector Craddock, arrives to question the suspects. Marty appears innocent, intent only on business. Lola once had an affair with Jason and has previously attempted to shoot Marina but it was Jason's secretary, Ella Zielinsky, who gave Marina the coffee. However, she too is murdered.

Fully recovered Miss Marple believes that the vital clue lies in Marina's conversation with Heather.

GW Films

Discovering this she solves the case — Marina's long illness began when the child she had always wanted was born mentally handicapped, Heather had been infectious with German measles when they had met. It was Marina who murdered Heather and doctored the evidence to point to herself as the intended victim. Aware of this Jason has provided his wife with a poisoned hot drink and Miss Marple finds Marina dead.

"What you buy your tickets for, the makers undoubtedly hope, is the gaudy galaxy of stars, all encouraged to Do Their Own Thing to the point of self-parody. Rock Hudson (as the movie's director) and Tony Curtis (producer) dispense polar brands of Hollywood machismo - Hudson strong-jawed and immovable as Mount Rushmore, Curtis mercurial and Brooklynite."

FINANCIAL TIMES

BRAINWAVES

U.S.A. 1982 – RUNNING TIME: 81 MINUTES
CINEAMERICA PRODUCTIONS

DIRECTOR:	ULLI LOMMEL	CAST	
PRODUCER:	ULLI LOMMEL		
EXECUTIVE PRODUCERS:	CHARLES APERIA,	KEIR DULLEA	JULIAN BEDFORD
	GARY GILLINGHAM AND	SUZANNA LOVE	KAYLIE BEDFORD
	TIM NIELSEN	VERA MILES	MARIAN
SCREENPLAY:	ULLI LOMMEL	PERCY RODRIGUES	DR. ROBINSON
ART DIRECTION:	STEPHEN E. GRAFF	TONY CURTIS	DR. CLAVIUS
DIRECTOR OF PHOTOGRAPHY:	JON KRANHOUSE	PAUL WILSON	DR. SCHRODER
	AND ULLI LOMMEL	RYAN SEITZ	DANNY BEDFORD
EDITOR:	RICHARD BRUMMER	NICHOLAS LOVE	WILLY MEISER
SOUND:	ED CHRISTIANO	CORINNE ALPHEN	LELIA ADAMS
	AND JOHN HUCK	EVE BRENT ASHE	MISS SIMPSON
PRODUCTION MANAGER:	RON NORMAN		
MUSIC:	ROBERT O. RAGLAND		

Director Ulli Lommel was one of Germany's most popular teenage actors, enjoying a productive association with the late Rainer Fassbinder, before turning director and gaining international acclaim for his feature 'The Tenderness of the Wolves' (1974). Since moving to America he has concentrated on horror films, usually employing his wife Suzanna Love, and found notable box-office success with 'The Boogey Man' (1980). The cast of 'Brainwaves' were quick to praise him and Curtis said; "He's amazing. I've never worked with anyone like him before. He only says one or two words, but he directs me with his eyes."

"Brainwaves" was filmed in San Francisco, Los Angeles and the Pettis Veterans Administration Hospital in Redlands during the Spring of 1982 and, when not required on set, Curtis could be found signing autographs and posing for pictures with patients and visitors. To date the film has not been seen in Britain.

San Francisco. Young housewife Kaylie Bedford is seriously injured in a hit and run car accident. She suffers a severe brain trauma and is left in a coma. Her husband Julian and mother Marion reluctantly agree to an experimental medical treatment which may produce a miracle cure. Noted neuro-scientist Dr Clavius promises to carry out his newly-developed 'Clavius Process' which transfers corrective patterns by computer from a donor brain to the damaged sections of Kaylie's brain. Unknown to Julian the process has not been tested on humans.

Kaylie stages a remarkable recovery and the 'Clavius Process' is hailed as an amazing medical breakthrough. When she returns home Kaylie is subject to a series of nightmares and hallucinations of a vivid murder and she becomes schizophrenic. Julian is reassured by the doctors that such side-effects are possible and that there is nothing to be alarmed about. He goes in search of his own solution trying to identify a song that Kaylie keeps repeating. After further tests Clavius admits that Kaylie has also registered the transference of some unknown thought processes and personality traits from the donor brain's owner.

Julian's research leads him to a Mrs. Simpson and he begins to piece together the case. He discovers that Kaylie has received the brain of a murdered girl and is now plagued by memories of the death which was classified by the police as an accident. The murderer, Willy Meiser, is also after Kaylie to prevent his discovery. With this information Julian is able to resolve the case and give his terrified wife peace of mind.

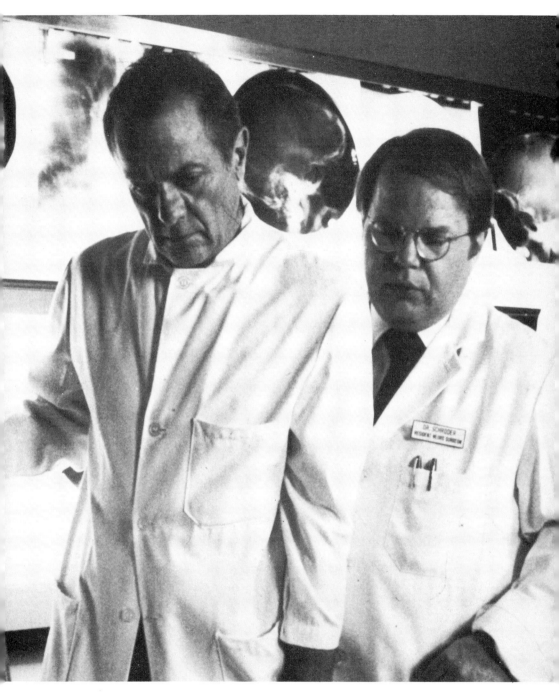

Paul Wilson   Cineamerica Productions

"Brainwaves is a briskly-told, engaging psychological thriller dealing with the sci-fi concept of transferring thought processes and memories electronically between different people. Well-edited by Richard Brummer, the picture zips along with admirable verisimilitude. Name players in the supporting cast (particularly a glum-looking Tony Curtis) have little to do."

VARIETY

OTHELLO – THE BLACK COMMANDO

FRANCE-SPAIN 1982 – RUNNING TIME: 103 MINUTES
A M.B. DIFFUSION EUROCINE PRODUCTION

		CAST	
DIRECTOR:	MAX H. BOULOIS		
PRODUCER:	MARIA J. GONZALEZ		
EXECUTIVE PRODUCER:	MARIA J. GONZALEZ	MAX H. BOULOIS	OTHELLO
SCREENPLAY:	MAX H. BOULOIS FROM THE PLAY	TONY CURTIS	IAGO
	BY WILLIAM SHAKESPEARE	RAMIRO OLIVEROS	CASSIO
DIRECTOR OF PHOTOGRAPHY:	DOMINGO SOLANO	JOANNA PETTET	DESDEMONA
EDITOR:	ANTONIO GIMENO	NADUISKA	GERARD BARRAY

'Othello —The Black Commando' is another highly suspect independent international production of the type that Curtis has chosen to associate himself with in recent years. He began work on the film during the late Spring of 1982, almost immediately after completing his role in 'Brainwaves'. The picture was made on locations in New York, Martinique and Spain. It has received scant public exposure since its completion and from the very few reviews that it has received the general impression given is that the whole enterprise is inept. The advertising for the film describes it as based on the William Sheakspeare (sic) classic.

Max H. Boulois is a Spanish resident expatriate from the Caribbean who had previously made an adventure film variously known as 'Black Jack' and 'Assault on a Casino'. It was his entire inspiration to make a contemporary reworking of Shakespeare and to employ Curtis and Joanna Pettet as his co-stars. Othello is now an American mercenary in Africa who is smitten by a Boston senator's daughter.

The respected industry journal 'Variety' summarised the plot as follows; "Item starts out as a commando actioner. A group of mercenaries overruns some African outpost (no dialog). They're accompanied by the Senator's prim daughter who falls for the husky black general, meanwhile a tired and ageing Iago (Tony Curtis) plants the seeds of doubt.

The commando group then moves to some Central American banana republic where the 'tragedy' comes to a head, after Cassio's accused of trying to rid the world of Othello, through Iago's scheming, and after two would-be soliloques Boulois throttles the gal, Iago bites the dust in a shoot-out and Othello commits suicide."

Variety went on to offer the following review; "Despite the numerous action scenes sprinkled throughout the film, the script, direction and editing are so rudimentary that none of it ever adds up to anything: pic has a fatal lack of continuity and an overriding feeling of improvisation."

The music for the film is provided by Beethoven's 5th and 9th Symphonies. The film has not been released in Britain and was unavailable for viewing by the author.

Max H. Boulois   M.B. Diffusion EUROCINE Production

BALBOA

U.S.A. 1982 – RUNNING TIME: 96 MINUTES
ENTERTAINMENT ARTISTS/PRODUCTION ASSOCIATES

		CAST	
DIRECTOR:	JAMES POLAKOF		
PRODUCER:	JAMES POLAKOF		
ASSOCIATE PRODUCERS:	JOHN CANNON	TONY CURTIS	ERNIE STODDARD
	AND NANCY JUDD	CAROL LYNLEY	ERIN BLAKELY
SCREENPLAY:	JAMES POLAKOF	JENNIFER CHASE	KATHY LOVE
ART DIRECTION:	CHARLES D. TOMLINSON	STEVE KANALY	SAM COLE
DIRECTOR OF PHOTOGRAPHY:	CHRISTOPHER LYNCH	CHUCK CONNORS	ALABAMA DERN
EDITOR:	MILLIE PAUL	LUPITA FERRER	RITA CARLO
SOUND:	ANTHONY SANTA CROCE	SONNY BONO	TONY CARLO
PRODUCTION MANAGER:	CAROL LAND	CATHERINE CAMPBELL	CINDY DERN
MUSIC:	RICHARD HIERONYMUS	CASSANDRA PETERSON	ANGIE STODDARD
COSTUMES:	NICKI LEWIS	DAVID YOUNG	LANCE ARMSTRONG
		HENRY JONES	JEFFREY DUNCAN

A hectically-plotted soap-opera with Curtis as the 'J.R. of the jet-set', Balboa made its only appearance in Britain on video during the summer of 1984. Among the cliche-characters not mentioned in the plot synopsis are oil-wealthy Texan Alabama Dern (Chuck Connors), and Rita Carlo (Lupita Ferrer) — a former child actress trying to make a movie comeback.

There is an abundance of material here for a television 'soap' but thankfully that possibility never materialised. The superfluity of female nudity and 'steamy' sex scenes would have had to be trimmed for primetime consumption in America. Among the glamorous locations used during the filming was the John Wayne Tennis Club. The generally vapid musical soundtrack includes the number 'Millionaire' sung by Leo Sayer.

A Narrator informs us that Balboa is the 'jet set playground of the wonderfully wealthy'. The local 'Mister Big' is Ernie Stoddard who tours the area in his luxury cruiser accompanied by his current 'companion' Kathy Love. A powerful man, Stoddard has many enemies including Cindy Dern, who wants revenge for Stoddard's financial ruin of her grandfather, Jeffrey Duncan, and Stoddard's ex-wife Angie, who is bitter over her paltry divorce settlement. The woman Stoddard genuinely loves is Erin, the widow of his partner Tom Blakely, but she remains immune to his charms happily courted by Sam Cole, an upright local politician.

For Stoddard business is paramount and his current concern is the success of his new gambling operation on Goat Island. Angie and Cindy combine to plot his downfall blackmailing his secretary Shirley into providing a file detailing illegal bribes. The material is handed over to Cole along with the confirmation that Stoddard had arranged Tom Blakeley's death. Stoddard has the area's senator in his power and avoids prosecution by discrediting his secretary's evidence. When Cole knocks him to the ground Stoddard is also able to press assault charges against the politician.

Triumphant again, Stoddard dispenses with Kathy Love and explains to Erin how he has been managing $500,000 trust fund for her daughter, planned with Tom. Cole has offered marriage to Erin but she has hesitated and must make a choice between Cole or Stoddard. Meanwhile Kathy Love has found a new rich protector in Stoddard's arch rival. The Narrator promises that 'the saga will continue'.

Jennifer Chase

Entertainment Artists/Production Associates

WHERE IS PARSIFAL?

UNITED KINGDOM 1984 - RUNNING TIME: 84 MINUTES
SLENDERLINE LTD/TERENCE YOUNG PRODUCTIONS

		CAST	
DIRECTOR:	HENRI HELMAN		
PRODUCER:	DANIEL CARRILLO		
EXECUTIVE PRODUCER:	TERENCE YOUNG	TONY CURTIS	PARSIFAL KATZENELLENBOGEN
SCREENPLAY:	BERTA DOMINGUEZ D.	CASSANDRA DOMENICA	ELBA
ART DIRECTION:	MALCOLM STONE	ERIK ESTRADA	HENRY BOARD II
DIRECTOR OF PHOTOGRAPHY:	NORMAN LANGLEY	PETER LAWFORD	MONTAGUE CHIPPENDALE
EDITOR:	RUSSELL LLOYD	RON MOODY	BEERSBOHM
	AND PETER HOLLYWOOD	DONALD PLEASENCE	MACKINTOSH
SOUND:	DAVID CROZIER	ORSON WELLES	KLINGSOR
PRODUCTION SUPERVISOR:	VINCENT WINTER	CHRISTOPHER CHAPLIN	IVAN
MUSIC:	HUBERT ROSTAING	NANCY ROBERTS	RUTH
	AND IVAN JULIEN		
COSTUMES:	MONICA HOWE		

At the time of writing Curtis's most recent film has yet to be released. Filmed in Britain during the late autumn of 1983 'Where is Parsifal?' is a comedy starring Curtis as hypochondriac inventor Parsifal Katzenellenbogen. From his castle he attempts to sell his latest invention; a laser skywriter, and holds a dinner party to try and attract the investment of tycoon Henry Board II. The screenplay is by Berta Dominguez D. who also acts in the film under the name of Cassandra Domenica.

The film received its world premiere at the 1984 Cannes Film Festival with Curtis in attendance. Variety reviewed the film from the Festival observing; "Where is Parsifal? is one of those pictures that makes one wonder how it got made at all." The reviewer continued; "it's all irrelevant to anything resembling entertainment." The final comment from Variety read; "it's a fiasco from start to finish."

OTHER WORKS

Apart from the films listed in full in the main text Curtis has also appeared as a guest star in several cameo roles. In 1960 he was one of numerous major stars to make a brief appearance in 'Pepe', a lengthy comedy with Cantinflas. Among the other box-office names were Maurice Chevalier, Bing Crosby, Jimmy Durante, Greer Garson, Jack Lemmon, Dean Martin and Frank Sinatra. Curtis and Janet Leigh were seen in one segment in which Leigh believes Cantinflas to be an important member of the Mexican censorship board who has arrived to discuss her film 'Passion' which is about to open south of the border. In reality he is acting as an agent for Dan Dailey and is attempting to persuade Leigh to co-star in a film.

Curtis also appeared in 'The List of Adrian Messenger' (1963) as one of a quintet of heavily-disguised stars designed to add a few red herrings to this John Huston directed thriller. Robert Mitchum is a crippled pensioner in a wheelchair, Burt Lancaster is a stout-hearted matron opposing fox-hunting, Frank Sinatra is a gypsy and Tony Curtis is an organ grinder. Kirk Douglas's company produced the film and Douglas also appeared in disguise within the film although he plays a more substantial role than his fellow stars. At one stage Elizabeth Taylor was also to have added her presence as a merchant seaman. Curtis makes a brief appearance in the romantic comedy 'Paris When It Sizzles' (1963). William Holden stars as a scriptwriter opposite Audrey Hepburn and Curtis appears in Holden's mind as the provisional casting for his plot writing. Curtis can be glimpsed during a gambling scene in 'Chamber of Horrors' (1966) and his vocal talents were employed on the hugely successful chiller 'Rosemary's Baby' (1968).

Before going to Hollywood in 1948 Curtis made several stage appearances including 'The Prince Who Learnt Everything Out of Books', 'Dear Ruth' and the lead in 'Golden Boy'. In 1973 he was seen in an unsuccessful pre-Broadway run of 'Turtlenecks' and in 1980 was in Neil Simon's 'I Ought To Be In Pictures' during its Los Angeles run.

Curtis has many varied talents; he is an accomplished artist, an art collector, a skilled fencer and has published one novel, 'Kid Andrew Cody and Julie Sparrow'. A highly enjoyable, Harold Robbins style piece of fiction the book did not fare well, which was surprising. He began his writing career during his sabbatical from film production in the 1970s. Initially he produced two fifty-five thousand word novels — 'Julie Sparrow' and Kid Andrew Cody'. He told reporters that he hoped to find a European publisher and that the first book had been written specifically to be filmed. He hoped to play Sparrow from the age of thirty-five to fifty. He said; "When I decided to start writing I picked up a couple of how-to books and couldn't believe the crap I read. Then, Irving Lazar (then his agent) sent me a journal by Somerset Maugham that hooked me — it's called 'A Writer's Notebook'. I rarely read novels, prefer reading Scientific American or some theoretical discussion about Plato. But in thirty years I have had incredible experiences making movies. I figure life gives me my research. Making all the movies I have has allowed me to experience twice the life of most people."

His book eventually appeared in 1977 and he claimed; "I wrote two separate books — one on Kid Andrew Cody and one on Julie Sparrow. After I completed the stories I shuffled them together like a deck of cards and wrote some additional stuff and combined them into one novel. I tried to tell a narrative and envisage the characters without embellishment. And I chose a period that didn't take any research — from 1922 to 1960. I could call on my experiences." He was asked what had led him to a new role as an author. He replied; "I'm a highly motivated person. I research life, I remember textures, recall era and I have a sense of what people are like. I wanted to put my ideas in concrete form. While I was living my personal life I was also living all those fantasies I was making in the movies. Look at all the people I've played, all those environments I've been in, all the stories I've heard. It's a tremendous background for writing fiction. So I asked myself why I couldn't write a book. To me, acting and writing are inter-related. All the arts are related to one another. It's a matter of projecting emotions. I can't distinguish the creative impulses of either one. Can't say that I enjoy one more than the other. You become like litmus paper, just using the colours you need to reflect the proper emotion and leave the rest to chance."

Curtis received two hundred and eighty thousand dollars for his first novel and seemed about to embark on a new career. In 1979 he announced a second novel called 'Star

The Prince Who Learnt Everything Out of Books (1947)

Struck'. "It's all about the Hollywood I knew as a Universal contract player and to make it realistic I'm using real names alongside the fictional ones. So I have Clark Gable eating in the studio commissary with a reporter and Fred Astaire and Cyd Charisse hurrying through their salads to get back to the set. I'm really enjoying writing this one." There was also talk of a third novel to be set in Britain. Hollywood seemed to be more interested in the possibility of Curtis producing a volume of tell-all memoirs, a suggestion he was quick to reject. In 1979 he said; "How could I do it? How could I betray all those confidences I've enjoyed over the years. If I did I'd never be able to look myself in the mirror again.

"They'd researched me thoroughly. I'll give them that. They had gone through my film career and said to each other: 'Do you realise this actor has worked with everyone from Robert De Niro to Jack Lemmon to Frank Sinatra to Cary Grant? Think of the marvellous stories he must have.' So the publishers sent a woman out from New York to talk to me. And she showed me this long list of people they knew I'd worked with. It even had Jack Benny on it. 'I never worked with Jack Benny', I said. 'Oh yes you did', she said. 'You did a radio show with him years ago.' And you know something — I'd completely forgotten. Yet I still have the gold cufflinks he gave me. It showed how thorough their research had been."

When he turned down the publisher's entreaties he also rejected a substantial sum of money. "I could have made over three quarters of a million dollars. They spelled it out for me. They would sit me down with four writers and a lot of tape recorders and the whole thing would be wrapped up in six day's time. I feel very strongly about violating confidences. Over the years people like Brando have treated me as a friend. Can you imagine their reactions if they suddenly found me writing about them in a book. There are quite enough people doing that without me joining the list — even if it would make me a fortune."

To date 'Kid Andrew Cody and Julie Sparrow' remains Curtis's only literary effort to appear in print. Later plans to film the book with Curtis making his directorial debut came to nothing. In 1984, following his hospital treatment, he announced that he had now completed a second novel and that his recent experiences had convinced him that he should now write an autobiography.

Curtis was a frequent visitor to television screens during the 1970s. In 1971 he consented to make his first series 'The Persuaders', opposite Roger Moore. In America the series flopped but was a big hit in Europe where several of the episodes were released as films. In 1971 Curtis was given an award by French 'Tele 7 Jours' as the most popular foreign actor of the year on French television. The series was made by British entrepeneur

With Marie Windsor (left) in Chamber of Horrors

Lew Grade and Curtis moved to London fired with enthusiasm. He described his character, Danny Wilde, as; "Someone very like myself. He's born and bred in the Bronx, knows the difference between truth and bullshit and is not taken in by the Establishment. The problem with sustaining a character over twenty-four episodes is that there has to be room for development as well as identifiable mannerisms. I've added two to the script: I always try to get in close to people when I talk to them and I always keep my gloves on no matter what I'm doing." When 'The Persuaders' met with a cool reception in America and was not to be renewed Curtis analysed the problems; "I hoped the episodes would be written by many more than the eight or ten writers. The did not have enough American writers. This meant that I was speaking un-American idiom with an American accent and put in un-American situations. For example, I had to say: 'Give me the gat, I am a gangster'. No American gangster says that. It was as if Roger Moore owned the company in which I was the major star. It was like making me Prime Minister without Portfolio. The series lacked a spine. Every episode should have been different: should have had the audience guessing what was to happen next. It was a cartoon. A Batman. There were mythical men chasing mythical spies all over mythical countries with mythical daughters of mythical feathers turning chemicals into gold out of water."

In 1975 he made a short-lived Mystery Movie series for American television called 'McCoy' in which he played a con-man. The series took him back to Universal Studios where he had begun his career; "Rock Hudson and I are about the only ones left on the lot from those days", he said. "We only made theatrical films then but nowadays most of the activity comes from television. They try to make a difference between the two and there is none. 'McCoy' is perfect casting for me. I mean anybody who survives for twenty-five years in Hollywood must be a con-man." A few years later Curtis had a recurring role as casino owner Bernie Roth in the popular series 'Vegas' which starred Robert Urich. He said; "I know Vegas very well and I always liked it. It's nice to be able to guest star occasionally in the TV series because its a place I've had a lot of fun in."

In 1978 he appeared in the television film 'The Users' based on a book by former gossip columnist Joyce Haber which starred Jaclyn Smith, Joan Fontaine, John Forsythe and Red Buttons. In recent years he has made several television films; in 'Moviola' (1980) he gave an Emmy-nominated performance as David O. Selznick, he was a flamboyant gangster in 'Inmates: A Love Story' (1981) starring Kate Jackson and Shirley Jones and, in 'The Million Dollar Face' (1981) he was the head of a cosmetics firm in ruthless competition with another firm run by his former lover played by Lee Grant. Others in the cast included Sylvia Kristel and Roddy McDowall. The production was based on the novel

Jaclyn Smith and John Forsythe in The Users   The Kobal Collection

'Kiss Inc.' by Lois Wyse and it was seen as the forerunner to a possible series which never materialised.

The following is a selective list of his television appearances adapted from the book 'Actors' Television Credits' by James Robert Parish. He has also made various guest appearances in shows like 'Rowan and Martin's Laugh-In' and on chat shows like the British 'Parkinson' and 'Aspel and Company'.

1957	'Cornada' (episode of General Electric Theatre)
1958	'Man on a Rock' (episode of Schlitz Playhouse of Stars)
1959	'The Stone' (episode of General Electric Theatre)
1960	'The Young Juggler' (episode of Ford Star Time)
1965	'The Flintstones' (voice only)
1969	'Fade-In' (episode of Bracken's World)
1971	'The Persuaders' (series)
1973	'The Third Girl from the Left' (Television Movie with Kim Novak)
	'Shaft' (appearance in one episode)
1975	'The Big Rip-Off' (pilot for McCoy series)
	'McCoy' (series)
1978	'Vegas' (TVM and subsequent series)
	'The Users' (TVM)
1980	'Moviola: The Scarlett O'Hara War' (TVM)
1981	'The Million Dollar Face' (TVM)
	'Inmates: A Love Story' (TVM)
1984	'The Golden Land' (British documentary on Jews in America)

BOOKS

Bacall, Lauren	**'By Myself'** (UK. Jonathan Cape, 1979)
Balatke, Joe	**'The Films of Jack Lemmon'** (USA. Citadel Press, 1977)
Cottrell, John	**'Laurence Olivier'** (UK. Weidenfeld & Nicolson, 1975)
Curtis, Tony	**'Kid Andrew Cody and Julie Sparrow'** (UK. W.H. Allen, 1977)
Fitzgerald, Michael G.	**'Universal Pictures'** (USA. Arlington House, 1977)
Harbinson, W.A.	**'Bronson'** (UK. W.H. Allen, 1976)
Parish, James Robert & Bowers, Ronald L.	**'The MGM Stock Company'** (USA. Arlington House, 1973)
Poitier, Sidney	**'This Life'** (UK. Hodder & Stoughton, 1980)
Quinlan, David	**'The Illustrated Guide to Film Directors'** (UK. B.T. Batsford, 1983)
Shaw, Arnold	**'Sinatra—Retreat of the Romantic'** (UK. W.H. Allen, 1968)
Shipman, David	**'The Great Movie Stars'** (UK. Angus & Robertson, 1972)
Steinberg, Cobbett	**'Reel Facts'** (UK. Penguin Books, 1981)
Thomas, Tony	**'The Films of Kirk Douglas'** (USA. Citadel Press, 1972)

ARTICLES

Bentley, Jack	**'Why Tony Wakes Up Screaming'** (Sunday Mirror, 27/4/69)
Billington, Michael	**'Tony Curtis'** (The Times, 18/9/71)
Cashin, Fergus	**'The Sweet One'** (Daily Sketch, 4/7/65)
Christy, George	**'The Great Life'** (Hollywood Reporter, May 1978)
Devlin, Tim	**'Call Me Mister: The Seventh Age of Tony Curtis'** (The Times, 25/6/73)
Gardner, Barry	**'When Love Died for Tony Curtis'** (Daily Star, 9/11/82)
Gordon, George	**'Curtis. . .by the wife who never was'** (Daily Mail, 27/5/84)
Lewis, Richard Warren	**'The Story of Tony Curtis'** (Photoplay, November 1969)
Mann, Roderick	**'I Dress to Suit My Seven Cars Says Tony Curtis'** (Sunday Express, 10/10/65)
	'That Girl in the See-Through Blouse' (Sunday Express 27/5/79)
	'Terrible Times for Tony' (Sunday Express, 29/6/80)
Munn, Mike	**'Tony Curtis Is Back'** (Film Review, April 1975)
	'The Day Curtis Won't Forget' (Photoplay, March 1979)
Ottaway, Robert	**'How The Strangler Changed My Life'** (Daily Sketch, 27/6/69)
Owen, Michael	**'The Bronx's Gift to Belgravia'** (Evening Standard, 18/10/74)
Salisbury, Lesley	**'Why Curtis Feels Bitter'** (TV Times, 26/6/82–2/7/82)
Willows, Terry	**'Curtis Weds No 4 in Secret'** (Daily Star, 1/5/84)
	'Curtis Turning Over a New Leaf as Author' (Photoplay, October 1977)
	'Curtis Battles for his Sanity' (Sun, 8/4/80)
	'It's Now or Never says sick Curtis' (The Standard, 4/4/84)
	'Tony Curtis in Hospital Scare' (Sun, 30/3/84)
	'Tony Curtis in Triple Pic Role' (Variety, 15/9/76)

INDEX